THE ART
AND CRAFT OF
WOODEN TOYS

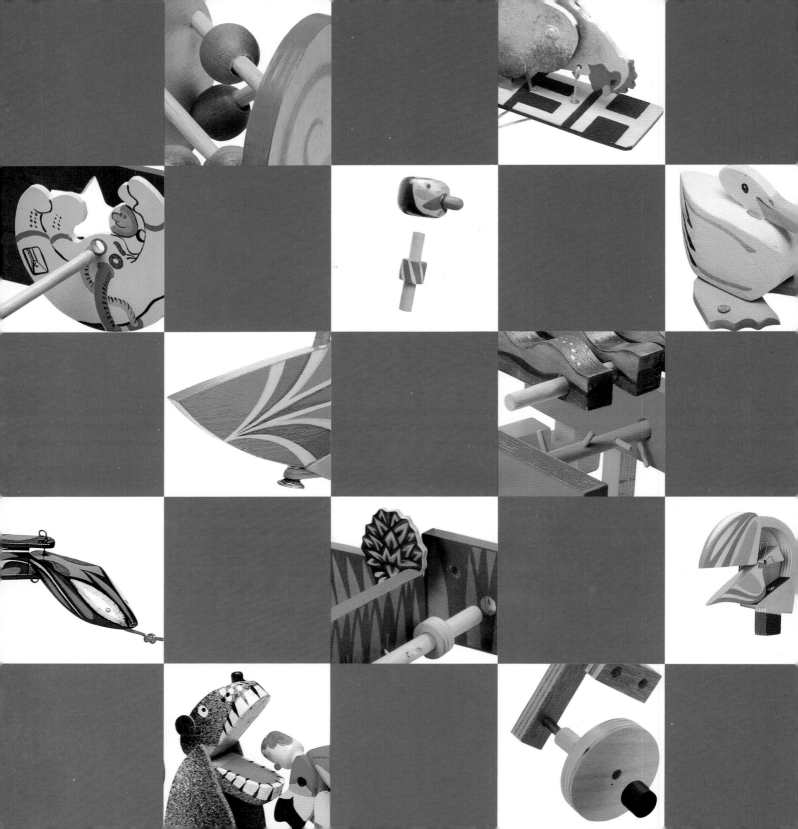

The Art
and Craft of
Wooden Toys

Ron Fuller
& Cathy Meeus

Running Press
Philadelphia, Pennsylvania

Library of Congress Cataloging-in-Publication Number 94-67759

Designed and produced by
Quarto Inc.
The Old Brewery
6 Blundell Street
London
N7 9BH

Senior editor **Maria Morgan**
Senior art editor **Mark Stevens**
Designer **John Grain**
Illustrators **Kuo Kang Chen, Carol Hill, David Kemp** (plans)
Photographers **Colin Bowling, Paul Forrester, Laura Wickenden**
Art director **Moira Clinch**
Editorial director **Sophie Collins**

Typeset by Genesis Typesetting, Rochester, Kent
Manufactured in Hong Kong by Regent Publishing Services Ltd
Printed in China by Leefung-Asco Printers Ltd

CONTENTS

· INTRODUCTION ·

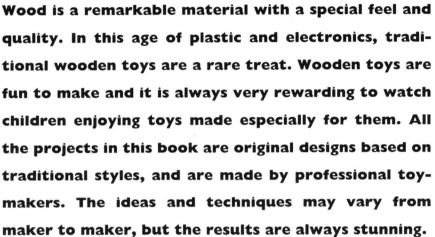

Wood is a remarkable material with a special feel and quality. In this age of plastic and electronics, traditional wooden toys are a rare treat. Wooden toys are fun to make and it is always very rewarding to watch children enjoying toys made especially for them. All the projects in this book are original designs based on traditional styles, and are made by professional toy-makers. The ideas and techniques may vary from maker to maker, but the results are always stunning.

Whether you are a complete woodworking novice or a skilled craftsperson, the clear and concise illustrated step-by-step instructions will allow you to develop and improve your skills. The first part of the book outlines the materials, tools, and equipment you will need and takes you through the basic techniques used in the projects. A basic tool-kit found in most households is really all you need, and this lively assortment of colorful toys, puzzles and moving figures is guaranteed to inspire and encourage you. Work your way through the book, or choose projects to suit your family and friends.

· HOW TO USE THIS BOOK ·

The first part of the book deals with materials and equipment and basic techniques used in the projects. The basic principles needed to make the toys are illustrated and include: scaling up and transferring designs; choosing and using wood and other materials; cutting and drilling; gluing; painting and varnishing. There are then 19 projects to make, presented in the following format.

The first spread includes a photograph, a brief introduction to the toy, and the specific materials and equipment needed to make it.

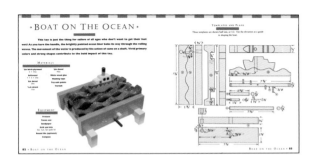

Stage One

The spread also gives complete templates and plans for the project, including the scale where not shown full-size.

All component parts are listed by number, name, and type of material for easy reference.

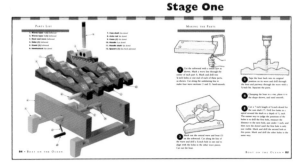

Stage Two

The positioning of the components is shown in a unique "exploded" photograph, with numbers corresponding to the parts list. While colored here, check

which parts are actually painted before assembly.

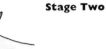

These are the fully illustrated step-by-step instructions for making the project.

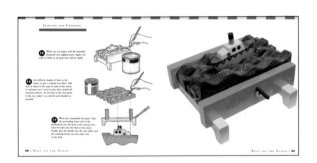

Stage Three

The final page shows a large, full-color photograph of the finished toy.

·Equipment and Materials·

The projects in this book can be undertaken by anyone with a basic knowledge of woodworking. They require a minimum of tools and equipment, and the materials are all readily available from hardware, arts and crafts, and model airplane stores.

Equipment

The largest item you will need is a sturdy workbench. A home-made wooden bench is ideal. However, a portable workbench of the type used for hobby work in the home is perfectly adequate. It is important to have a good-quality woodworking vise with wooden jaws. If you have one with metal jaws, you can adapt it by screwing two pieces of ½ inch plywood to the inside of the vise. A bench hook is useful for steadying items that cannot be held in a vise.

The tools and equipment you need in addition to your workbench and vise are listed at the start of each project. The list on the right summarizes the items common to most projects. The most essential tools are indicated with a bullet ●. The emphasis is on simple hand tools, but if you have more sophisticated power tools, these can, of course, be used.

Basic Tool Kit

- ● Tenon saw
- ● Fretsaw and cutting table
- Coping saw
- Hacksaw
- Small hacksaw
- Chisels
  ½in and ¼in
- ● Craft knife
- ● Smoothing plane
- ● Block plane
- ● Small hammer
- ● Mallet
- Rasp
- Sandpaper
- Flat and round metal files
- Ordinary pliers
- ● Round-nosed pliers
- Needle-nosed pliers

- Wire cutters
- Metal snips
- ● Screwdrivers
  (slotted and Phillips)
- ● Power drill and drill stand
- ● Selection of high-speed and spade bits
- Countersink bit
- ● Mini drill chuck
- Hole saws
- ● C-clamps
- ● Long ruler
- Square
- Soldering iron and general purpose solder
- Scissors
- Protractor
- Tool compass

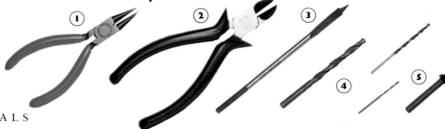

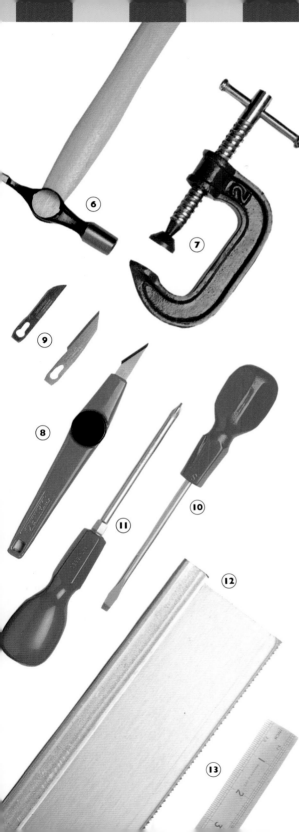

Plywood

Plywood made from thin layers of wood is one of the main materials for the maker of wooden toys. Birch plywood from Finland or Russia is the most commonly used, although Ramin and mahogany plywood are used for some projects. Always choose the best quality available – grade BB – in which both sides are smooth and almost knot-free.

Plywood is available in a variety of thicknesses. For the projects in this book the sizes used are ⅛ inch, ¼ inch, ⅜ inch and ½ inch.

Aircraft-grade plywood

Available in 1/16 inch thickness, this is a flexible plywood used extensively for model-making and is available from model airplane hobby stores.

Softwood

Usually pine, this easily obtainable category of wood is used in many projects in this book where a solid piece of wood is required. Select wood that is knot-free and that has a consistent close grain. Maple can be substituted, but it is more expensive and sometimes hard to find except in hardwood lumber yards.

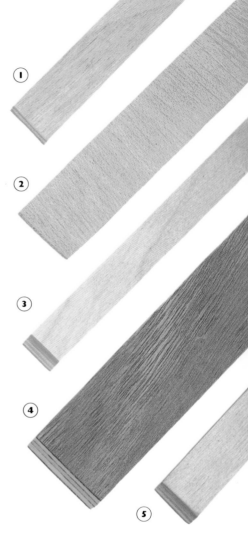

Equipment

1 Needle-nosed pliers; **2** round-nosed pliers; **3** spade bit; **4** high-speed bits **5** countersink bit; **6** pin hammer; **7** C-clamp; **8** blades; **9** craft knife; **10** slotted screwdriver; **11** Phillips screwdriver; **12** tenon saw; **13** steel ruler.

Plywood

1 Birch; **2** aircraft-grade plywood; **3** ramin; **4** mahogany; **5** plywood;

Softwood is sold in "nominal" sizes. This means that if you buy a length of surfaced wood, the size you are actually given will be approximately ⅛ inch smaller all around. The instructions in this book refer to the nominal size, but to save yourself the trouble of planing, always select surfaced wood.

Dowels

Dowels are used extensively in toymaking for pivots, shafts, and spacers. Where a dowel is specified, birch is the preferred wood because it is easy to work with, has a pleasing appearance, and is most easily obtained from arts and craft stores. Before buying, check the dowel for roundness as sometimes faults in the cutting process creates an oval or stepped section that could create a problem in making a toy. Ramin dowels are more difficult to work with and are therefore a less satisfactory alternative.

Dowels are available in a range of diameters. The usual sizes are ⅛ inch, 3/16 inch, ¼ inch, ⅜ inch, and ½ inch. Like all wood measurements, the size you buy may not be completely accurate. It may therefore be necessary to adjust the dowel thickness by sanding, in order to ensure that it fits to the degree of tightness required. Similarly, if you cannot obtain the precise size you need, it may be possible to buy the next size up and sand down to fit.

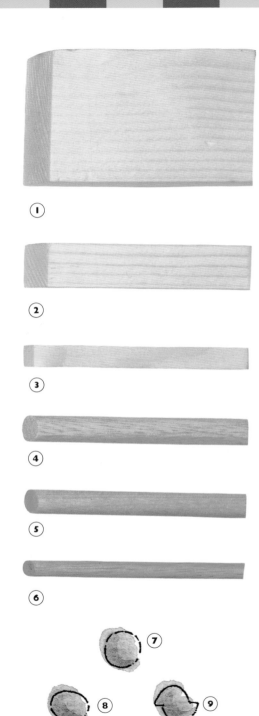

Wood and dowel

1 Softwood; **2** pine; **3** beech; **4 5 6** dowels; **7** round dowel; **8** oval dowel; **9** irregular dowel.

Screws, nails, and glues

1 Screws; **2** brads; **3** gimp tacks; **4** eye screws; **5** white wood glue; **6** rapid-drying epoxy; **7** contact cement; **8** superglue.

SCREWS, NAILS, AND GLUES

Screws

There is a huge variety of screw types to choose from, and selection is largely a matter of personal preference. They are available in different lengths and gauges (expressed as a numbered size) to fit different sizes of drilled holes. In this book, most of the screws used are countersunk, that is, they have a flat head that when inserted in a suitably drilled hole, will lie flush to the surface. Phillips head screws are usually easier to tighten. The newest screw designs, which have a dual thread that goes in more smoothly and grips more firmly are generally preferable. Whatever type of screw you are using, it is important to use a compatible screwdriver with a good blade to avoid damage to the screw head which could spoil the appearance.

Brads and gimp tacks

Brads of various sizes and gauges are often used in addition to glue to secure an assembly. They can be brass or steel. For toymaking, it is best to use the thinnest gauge available. Gimp tacks are large-headed brass tacks or mild steel pins used in upholstery. They are specified in some projects where a decorative effect is desired, but if you cannot obtain them, steel brads will serve just as well.

Glues

Four types of glue are used in the projects in this book.

White wood glue. This is a general-purpose glue that is applied only to one of the surfaces to be joined. Wipe away any excess with a damp cloth immediately. Choose the type that is fast-grab and quick-drying which can be obtained from arts and crafts stores. White wood glue can be thinned for gluing paper with an equal volume of water.

Rapid-drying epoxy glue. This is supplied in two parts – adhesive and hardener – that have to be mixed in equal parts before use. It has good filling properties and provides a strong bond for metal and wood.

Contact cement. Providing a strong and immediate bond, this glue should be applied to both surfaces and left for ten minutes before joining the parts.

Superglue. A useful adhesive for small parts that cannot easily be supported for long periods of drying, utmost care must be taken not to allow the glue to come into contact with skin or eyes.

Use fine synthetic watercolor brushes for all detail work. They are soft but durable and are available in a variety of sizes. Make sure that you only buy good-quality brushes. For painting large areas, use a natural or synthetic oil-painting brush.

OTHER MATERIALS

Metal parts

Some toys use small metal parts in addition to the main wooden structure. Tin and brass sheets are sometimes specified and can be obtained in small quantities from arts and crafts stores, as can brass rods and piano wire. As an alternative to buying new tin sheets, you can use scrap metal from a discarded square can, for example, of cooking oil.

Plastic and acrylic

Plastic washers are a lightweight alternative to metal washers and have the advantage that you can drill the hole to the precise size you require. They are easily made from the type of hard plastic used for supermarket milk and juice containers. Clear acrylic sheet used for windows are available from arts and crafts stores and plastics suppliers.

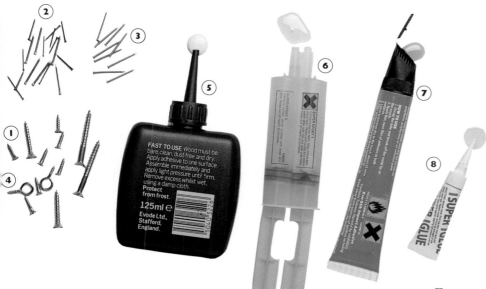

· BASIC TECHNIQUES ·

While this is not intended to be a comprehensive guide to all woodworking techniques, on the following pages you will find some useful general hints on the specific woodworking and toymaking techniques used in this book. It is advisable to read this section carefully before starting the projects. Use it also as a reference while working.

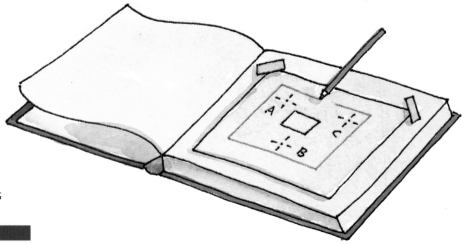

MAKING AND USING TEMPLATES

Most of the projects in this book provide diagrams for you to use to create your own templates for the pieces that make up each toy. Wherever possible these are shown full size to avoid the necessity of scaling up the diagrams.

The usual method for transferring the designs to the wood is to trace the diagram from the book, making sure that you include all the information, including positions of drill holes and position guides for later assembly.

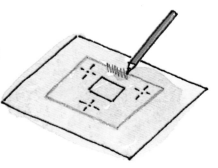

Turn the tracing paper over and shade over the reverse side of the marks with a soft pencil.

Tape the tracing paper right side up to the surface of the wood and draw over the original pencil lines using firm pressure to transfer the marks to the wood. Use a pointed tool such as the end of a compass to mark the centers of the drill holes. Remove the tracing paper and mark any further information you may need – such as reference numbers or bit sizes – on the wood.

If you wish to make a longer-lasting template that you can use again, instead of transferring the traced design directly onto the wood, transfer it onto posterboard. Cut around the edge of the design. Attach this to the wood with double-sided tape and draw around the edge in pencil. Mark hole positions through the template with a sharp point, as before.

SCALING UP

Where the plans and templates are not given full size, a scale or ratio is given. Full size (100 percent) has a ratio of 1 to 1, written as 1:1; half-size (50 percent) is 1:2, two-thirds (66.7 percent) is 2:3 and so on. Use the following calculations to scale up the plans:

1:2 = ÷ by 1 × by 2 or enlarge on a photocopier to 200%; **3:4** = ÷ by 3 × by 4 or enlarge to 133.3%; **2:3** = ÷ by 2 × by 3 or enlarge to 150% To work out the enlargement percentage: (scale 2:3) 3/2 × 100 = 150%; (scale 3:4) 4/3 × 100 = 133.3%, and so on.

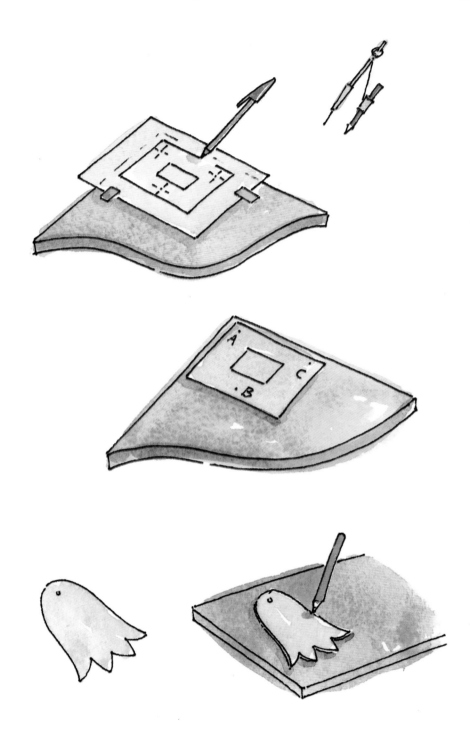

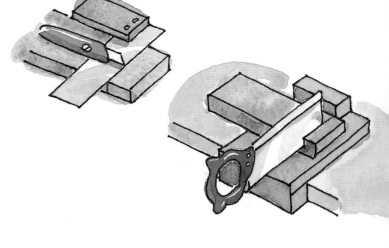

CUTTING SOFTWOOD

Use a tenon saw for straight cuts in softwood. For saw cuts in the direction of the grain, hold the wood in a vise or with C-clamps on a bench and follow a pencil line.

For saw cuts across the grain, mark the cut with a square and craft knife all the way around the wood. This helps to reduce ragged edges along the cut. Rest the wood against a bench hook while you cut.

CUTTING SLOTS IN SOFTWOOD

Mark all the way around the wood with a pencil (for a slot with the grain) or with a craft knife (for a slot across the grain), using a square for accuracy. Use a tenon saw to make parallel cuts to the depth marked. Use a coping saw to remove the waste.

The hand fretsaw, used for cutting plywood shapes, is one of the most important tools for the toymaker. It can be fitted with blades of different thicknesses according to the thickness of plywood to be cut. Unless specified otherwise in the instructions, use a medium blade for all the projects in this book. It is generally used in conjunction with a cutting table clamped to the edge of the workbench, which supports the sheet of plywood while you work.

To cut out shapes marked from the edge of the plywood, support the work on the cutting table with the edge to be cut facing you. Saw toward the bench, following the marked line. Turn the work as necessary so that you are always cutting in the same direction.

To cut holes or shapes from inside a sheet of plywood, drill a $\frac{1}{16}$ inch hole through the marked line of the hole. Remove the blade from the fretsaw and thread it through the hole. Reconnect it and saw along the marked lines as above.

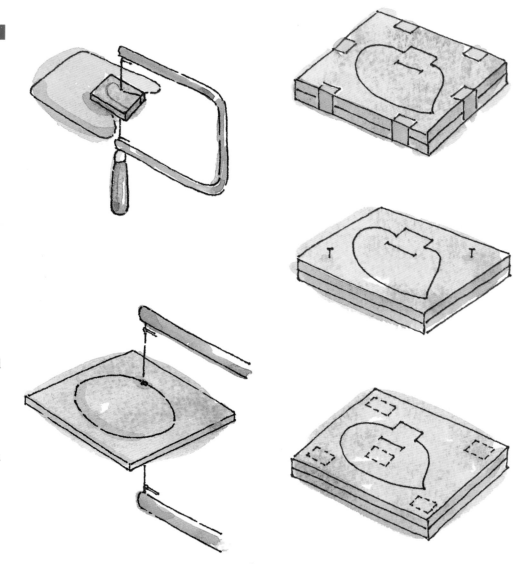

DRILLING

Throughout this book it has been assumed that the reader has a simple electric hand drill. Such a drill is perfectly suitable for all the drilling tasks required in these projects. However, it is strongly recommended for safety and accuracy that it is used in a drill stand with a built-in depth gauge and vise. For small holes requiring very fine bits, you need to fit a mini drill chuck to your drill.

GENERAL DRILLING HINTS

Unless the instructions specify otherwise, it is advisable to drill holes in plywood before cutting out the individual pieces. For holes at right angles to the surface, clamp the work horizontally in the vise and drill in the normal way. If you need to drill an angled hole, mark the intended path of the hole on the side of the work and align this vertically with the bit. When accuracy of angle is particularly critical, you may need to make a jig, as described in the Rolling Rattle (page 46).

Whenever you are drilling through a piece of work, place a piece of scrap plywood underneath to protect the bit and reduce fraying.

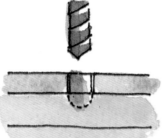

DRILLING TO DEPTH

To drill a hole to a specific depth, you normally simply set the depth gauge on your stand to the required amount. If you do not have one, or if the drill needs to be set too far from the work, you can mark the drill bit with masking tape to indicate the depth of the hole. You can then stop drilling when that point is reached.

DRILLING TO WIDTH

In toymaking, holes are drilled for a number of purposes and it is important to be aware of the reason for the hole before you start work. The hole may be to accommodate a turning dowel or rod, it may be for a dowel that needs to be a tight fit, or it may be a screw hole (see below). Be sure to select the right width bit for the job. For holes that are designed for a loose fit, for example, for the axles of a wheeled toy, you will notice that the instructions generally specify a bit size that is somewhat larger than the diameter of the dowel or rod it needs to accommodate. For holes in which a dowel is intended to fit tightly, greater accuracy is required and you should use a bit that is precisely the same size as the dowel or rod. If in doubt, choose a bit that is slightly smaller than you think may be needed. It is easier to enlarge a hole or

sand down the dowel to fit than it is
to compensate for a hole that has been
drilled too large.

SELECTING THE RIGHT BIT

For most kinds of drilling, use
standard high-speed bits. For holes
bigger than ¼ inch, spade bits give a
cleaner finish. A hole created with a
spade bit should be drilled from both
sides. Drill one side until the pointed
tip just starts to protrude. Then turn
the work and, using the hole as a
guide, drill from the other side. Brad-
point bits, originally designed for
industrial purposes, are now widely
available for the home market. They
produce a clean hole and are used in
the same way as spade bits.

RECESSED HOLES

To drill a hole that is larger on one
side than the other, first drill a hole of
the larger size with a spade or brad-
point bit to the required depth. Drill
the smaller second hole centered on
the first hole in the usual way.

HOLE SAWS

These are used to cut extra-large holes
and can be used to cut out wheels
without the need for a lathe. Available
in a number of diameters, the hole
saws fit into the chuck of a standard
drill. Prepare for drilling with a hole
saw by using a compass to draw the
size of circle you need. Unless you
need the hole to be in a specific
position, make sure that the rim of the
circle just touches the edge of the
wood. Drill a ¼ inch hole through the
center of the circle using a standard
high-speed bit. Attach a hole saw of
the required size to the drill and locate
the central bit in the previously drilled
hole. Drill halfway through the work
and then turn and complete the
drilling. Note that drilling with a hole
saw creates a lot of torque, so be sure
to secure your work firmly, by
clamping if possible.

DRILLING SCREW HOLES

The size of bit needed for screws holes is determined by the gauge of the screw. You need to drill the hole twice. The first drilling is to the length of the screw and uses a bit that is slightly smaller than the thread. This allows the screw to "bite" into the wood. Most woodworkers learn to judge this by eye. The second drilling uses a bit that is a fraction larger than the size of the shank and is drilled to the estimated depth of the unthreaded section. Careful drilling of screw holes in this way ensures a firm fit in which the screw does not split the wood as it is inserted.

COUNTERSUNK HOLES

Some screws are designed to be countersunk, that is to lie flush to the surface of the wood. To achieve this, drill the top section of the hole a third time using a countersink bit. Judge the depth of countersink by eye, test by inserting the screw, and drill again if necessary.

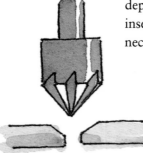

CUTTING DOWELS

Mark the length of dowel required with a craft knife, and complete the cut with a small hacksaw. Thin dowels may be cut all the way through with a craft knife.

CHAMFERING DOWELS

To ease the fit of a dowel into a hole, chamfer the end using a craft knife in the same way as you would sharpen a pencil. Smooth the end by rolling the dowel across a block of medium sandpaper.

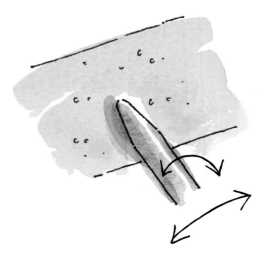

CHAMFERED AND BEVELED EDGES

An accurate chamfered, or sloping, edge on softwood should be marked with a pencil line along the edge of the wood, using a protractor and adjustable square as a guide. Holding the wood in a vise, use a block plane to remove the waste wood.

To cut mitered or beveled corners in plywood, mark the wood as above, using a craft knife to reduce fraying. Support the wood against a bench hook and cut along the mark with a small hacksaw.

SANDING

For a professional finish, it is important to keep your work smooth and free from frayed edges by sanding at regular stages. Keep four grades of sandpaper in stock for different kinds of sanding: coarse, medium, fine, and extra fine. They may be sold numbered 60, 100, 150, and 280 respectively. Each grade is suited for a different purpose. Use course sandpaper for shaping and reducing size. Medium is best for removing frayed edges after sawing and to smooth a surface after using coarse sandpaper. Use fine for sanding prior to painting. Extra fine sandpaper can be used as an alternative to steel wool for sanding down between coats of paint or varnish.

For ease of sanding flat surfaces and corners, make blocks of each grade of paper from scrap softwood. Round off two corners and wrap the sandpaper around the block. Secure at the back with a piece of scrap plywood, attached with brads, as shown. A triangular sanding block made from a wedge of softwood in a similar way is useful for sanding into corners. For sanding the insides of holes, wrap sandpaper around a length of dowel.

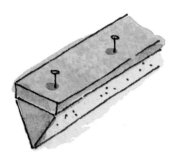

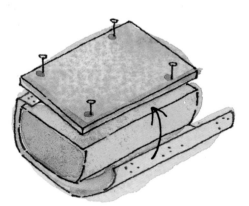

GLUING

For all gluing work make sure surfaces are clean and dust-free. Make sure that the room is well-ventilated as drying glue can give off fumes.

SOLDERING

A number of the projects have small metal parts that need to be joined by soldering. It is preferable to use a 40-watt soldering iron with general-purpose multicore solder recommended for electrical use. Clean metal surfaces to be joined with steel wool or extra fine sandpaper before soldering. Heat the joint well before applying the solder. Do not carry the solder to the joint with the iron as the flux will evaporate.

PAINTING

For painting wooden toys, you need durable paints that will not harm children if the toy is handled or sucked. For the best visual impact, you also need to select paints with strong, dense colors. There are a variety of paint options open to the toymaker. The paint you choose is to a large extent a matter of personal preference and availability.

Throughout this book the directions refer only to toy-safe paints, leaving you to decide by experimentation which materials suit you best.

Casein latex hobby paint. This is a water-based paint that dries to a water-resistant finish. For a more durable finish it should, however, be varnished. It has excellent covering properties and flows well for painting detail. It is a good choice for all projects where strong, flat color is preferred. It is available from well-stocked arts and crafts stores.

Oil-based enamel. Widely available from arts and crafts, and paint stores, these paints provide good coverage and are highly water resistant, even unvarnished. Use flat white enamel directly on the wood as an undercoat wherever an initial coat of white is specified. Detail may, however, be difficult to paint accurately with this type of paint.

Water-based dyes. In some cases, you may want to preserve the impression of wood. Water-based dyes, available in a variety of colors, allow the grain and character of the wood to show through. They can be applied in varying densities to produce a greater or lesser intensity of color. These cannot, however, be used for detail.

PAINTING TIPS

Sand all surfaces with fine sandpaper before painting. Make sure that the wood is clean and free from dust before any paint or dye is applied.

Unless you are using dyes, apply an undercoat of flat enamel paint before painting in the colour of your choice. To create a paper-like surface, apply two undercoats, rubbing down with steel wool between coats.

Where more than one coat of paint is needed, always allow the first coat to dry thoroughly and rub down with steel wool or extra fine sandpaper before applying the next coat.

USING SPRUES

Small toy parts may be difficult to handle while painting. You can often get around this problem by holding the pieces on a length of scrap dowel, known as a sprue, while you paint. Keep a selection of dowels of different widths approximately 4 inches long for this purpose. Chamfer the ends for ease of insertion into the part to be painted. For drying the painted parts, make a softwood sprue holder through which you have drilled a number of ¼-inch holes.

A fan heater set on low is useful for speeding up the drying process. Placing the toy, or toy part, in a

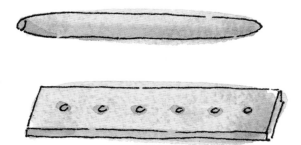

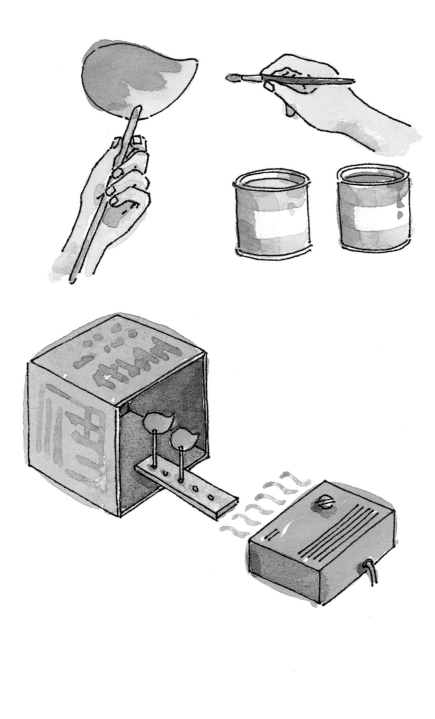

cardboard box will concentrate the warmth and cut down drying time even more. However, take care not to overheat the paint, which could cause cracking and may even warp the wood.

Varnish

Choose polyurethane varnish, which is hard-wearing and toy-safe. It is available in flat, satin, and gloss finishes and can be applied over paint or onto bare or dyed wood. For a durable finish, you need two coats of varnish. If you want to achieve an exceptionally deep shine or waterproofing, you may need a third coat of gloss varnish. Apply varnish with a flat synthetic brush about ½ inch wide. Do not use any brush for both paint and varnish. Allow the varnish to dry between coats, rubbing down with steel wool or extra fine sandpaper before each new application.

·UNDERWATER JIGSAW PUZZLE·

A traditional toy for every young child, this colorful jigsaw puzzle is perfect for encouraging hand-eye coordination and shape recognition. Because the pieces are thick enough to stand unsupported, a child can have hours of fun making underwater scenes from the pieces.

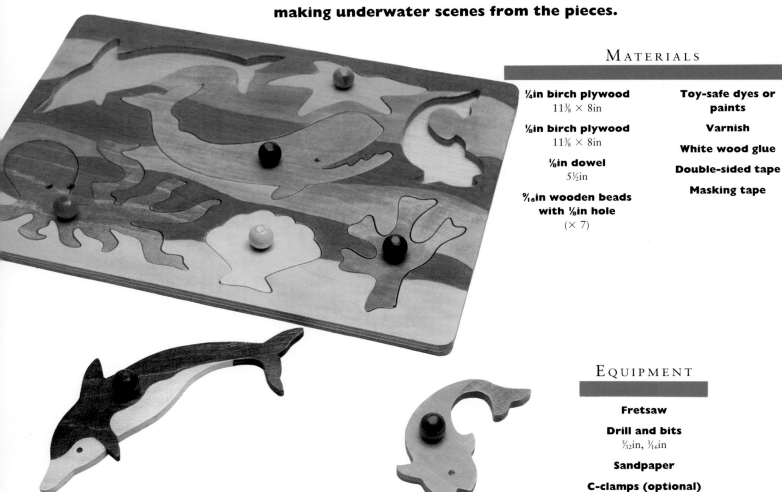

MATERIALS

¼in birch plywood
11⅜ × 8in

⅛in birch plywood
11⅜ × 8in

⅛in dowel
5½in

⁹⁄₁₆in wooden beads
with ⅛in hole
(× 7)

Toy-safe dyes or
paints

Varnish

White wood glue

Double-sided tape

Masking tape

EQUIPMENT

Fretsaw

Drill and bits
⁵⁄₃₂in, ¹⁄₁₆in

Sandpaper

C-clamps (optional)

Craft knife

Templates

The templates here are shown at 60 percent, or a ratio of 3:5, so scale
them up as necessary.

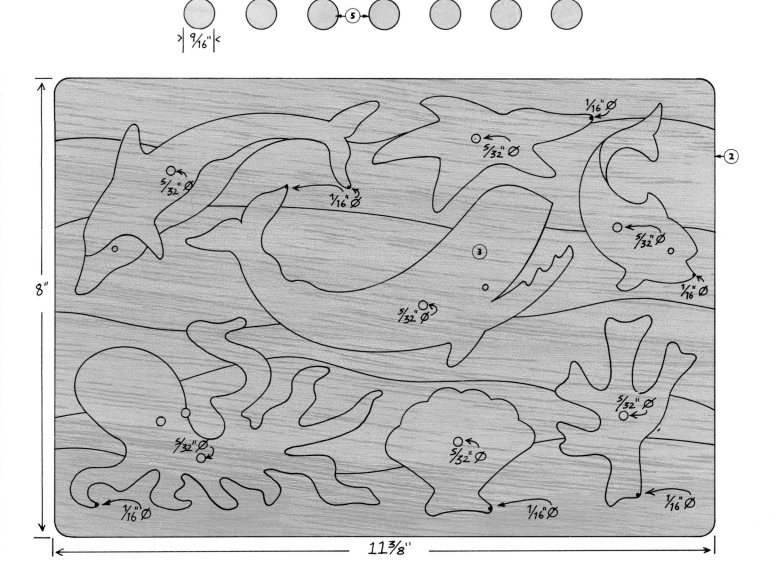

$\frac{9}{16}$"

5

$\frac{5}{32}$" ∅

$\frac{1}{16}$" ∅

$\frac{5}{32}$" ∅

$\frac{1}{16}$" ∅

2

$\frac{5}{32}$" ∅

3

$\frac{5}{32}$" ∅

$\frac{1}{16}$" ∅

$\frac{5}{32}$" ∅

$\frac{5}{32}$" ∅

$\frac{5}{32}$" ∅

$\frac{1}{16}$" ∅

$\frac{1}{16}$" ∅

$\frac{1}{16}$" ∅

8"

11$\frac{3}{8}$"

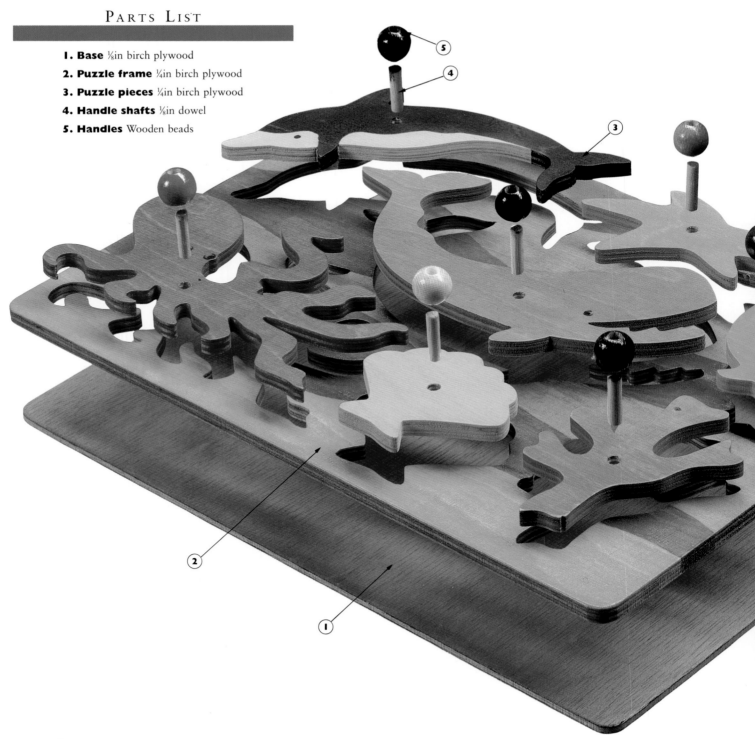

1. **Base** ⅛in birch plywood
2. **Puzzle frame** ¼in birch plywood
3. **Puzzle pieces** ¼in birch plywood
4. **Handle shafts** ⅛in dowel
5. **Handles** Wooden beads

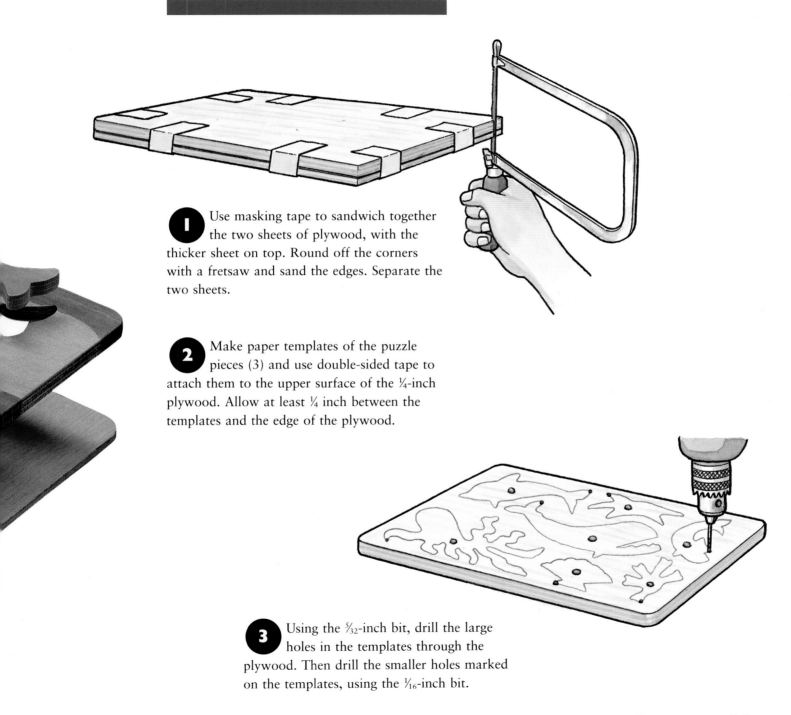

1 Use masking tape to sandwich together the two sheets of plywood, with the thicker sheet on top. Round off the corners with a fretsaw and sand the edges. Separate the two sheets.

2 Make paper templates of the puzzle pieces (3) and use double-sided tape to attach them to the upper surface of the ¼-inch plywood. Allow at least ¼ inch between the templates and the edge of the plywood.

3 Using the $\frac{5}{32}$-inch bit, drill the large holes in the templates through the plywood. Then drill the smaller holes marked on the templates, using the $\frac{1}{16}$-inch bit.

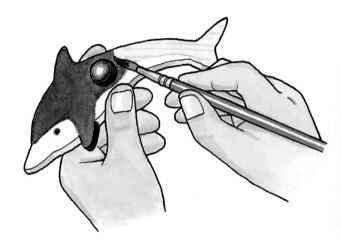

4 Using a fretsaw fitted with a fine blade, cut out the outline of each piece, following the direction indicated by the arrows on the templates. Lightly sand all pieces.

6 Paint or dye all pieces, including the background, as shown in the photographs, or in colors of your choice. Allow to dry.

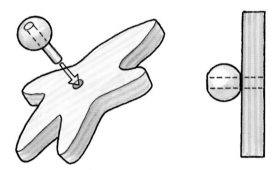

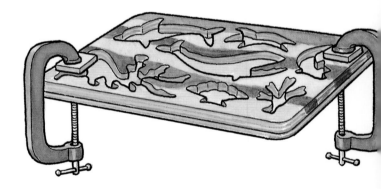

5 Cut the dowel into seven ¾-inch lengths. Glue a bead to one end of each piece, ensuring that the dowel extends all the way through the bead. Glue the other end of each dowel into the holes on the right side of each jigsaw shape. You may need to apply pressure in a vise to make sure that the dowel extends through the entire length of the hole so that the bead touches the surface of the piece. Wipe off any excess glue with a damp cloth.

7 Spread white wood glue thinly and evenly over the entire undersurface of the ¼-inch plywood. Press the two sheets of plywood together, making sure the edges are flush. Wipe away any excess glue immediately with a damp cloth. Tape or clamp the pieces together firmly until the glue is dry. Finally, apply two or three coats of varnish to all visible surfaces.

· SPACEWALKER ·

Its easy to imagine yourself taking a gentle spacewalk into the outer reaches of the galaxy with this wonderfully simple toy. Place the astronaut on one end of the frame and set him on his journey to the stars with a little tap. Now watch him roll rhythmically along the star-decorated frame until he comes to rest in the notches at the end.

EQUIPMENT

Fretsaw

Tenon saw

Coping saw

Drill and bit
¼in

Sandpaper

Craft knife

MATERIALS

¼in birch plywood
18 × 15in

⅛in birch plywood
4 × 4in

¼in dowel
4in

¾in softwood
18 × 2in

White wood glue

Toy-safe paints

Varnish

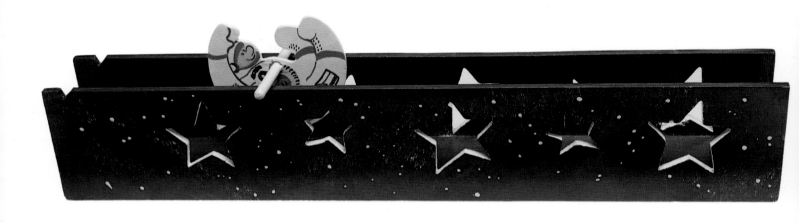

TEMPLATES AND PLANS

These templates are shown full size, with a cutting plan included below.

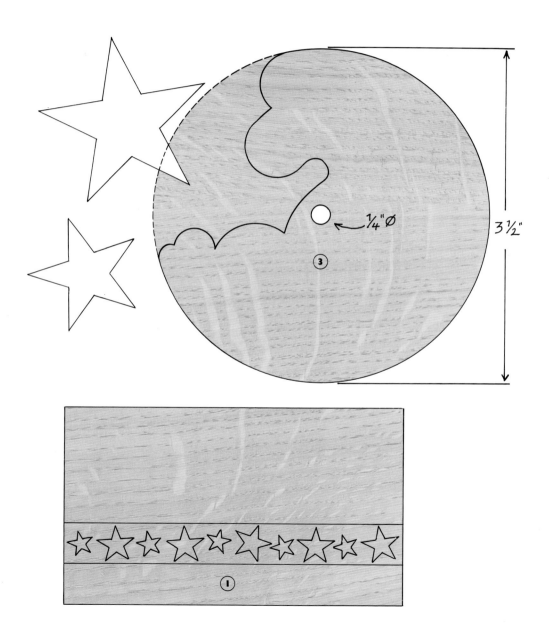

3½"

¼" Ø

③

①

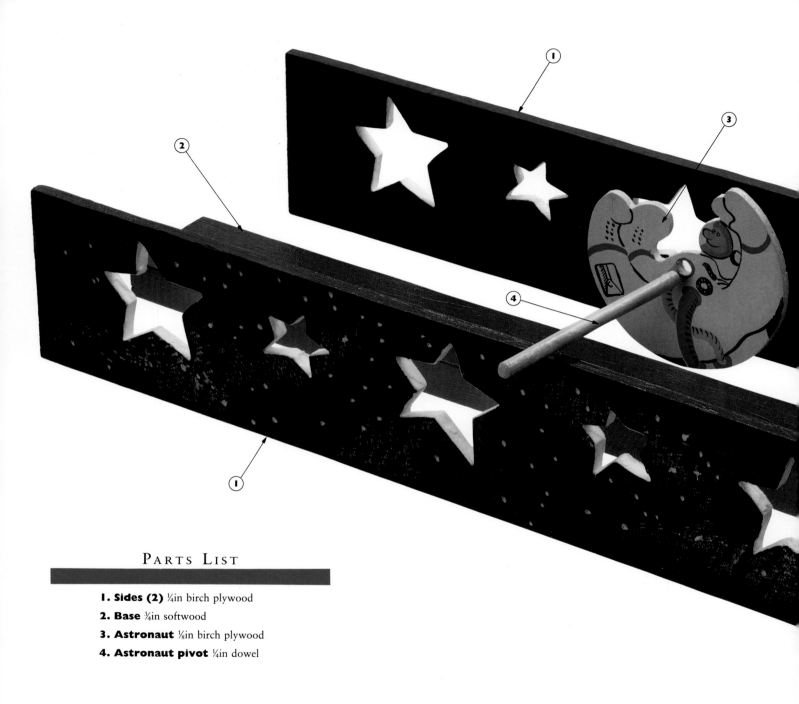

Parts List

1. **Sides (2)** ¼in birch plywood
2. **Base** ¾in softwood
3. **Astronaut** ⅛in birch plywood
4. **Astronaut pivot** ¼in dowel

1 Make a template for the astronaut (3) and mark it on the ⅛-inch birch plywood. Drill a hole with a ¼-inch bit in the position marked and then use a fretsaw to cut out the shape.

2 Mark two pieces measuring 3 × 18 inches on the ¼-inch birch plywood for the sides (1), and stick the two sides together with double-sided tape. Make templates from the star shapes and draw these onto one of the sides. Cut out the star shapes through both layers using a coping saw.

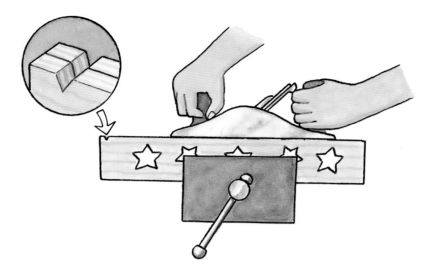

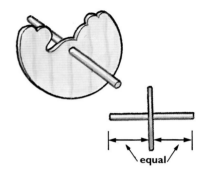

3 With the two sides still taped together, clamp them in a vise and cut a v-shaped notch in the top of both pieces with a tenon saw, about ½ inch from one end. Plane and sand all the straight edges until they are smooth. Separate the pieces.

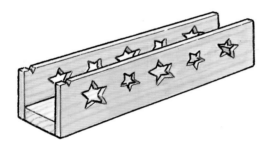

4 Glue the sides to the softwood base, making sure that the sides remain vertical and parallel.

5 Round off the ends of the dowel. Smear a little glue onto the middle of the dowel and push it through the hole in the astronaut so that the ends protrude equally on each side.

PAINTING THE PARTS

6 Give all the pieces two coats of white paint. When dry, paint the sides and the base in dark blue. Do not attempt to gain a uniform finish, but rather stipple and smudge the paint to create a more varied effect. While the paint is still wet, stipple some pink into some of the paler areas and some yellow into others. When the background is dry, add some extra distant stars with dots of white.

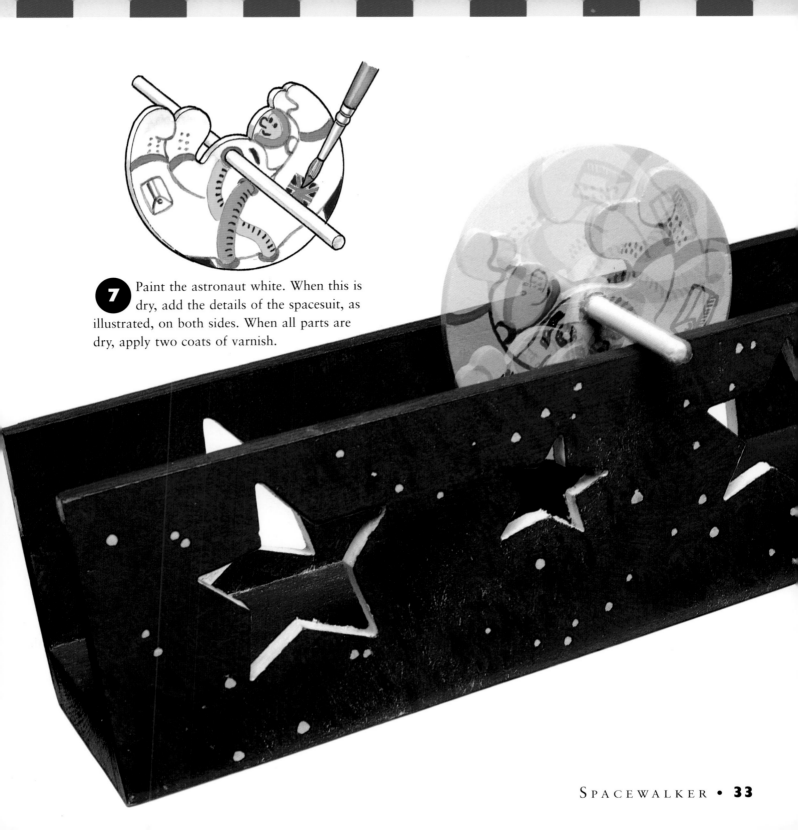

7 Paint the astronaut white. When this is dry, add the details of the spacesuit, as illustrated, on both sides. When all parts are dry, apply two coats of varnish.

· PULL-ALONG GIRAFFE ·

Here we have a miniature version of the popular pull-along toy. This intricately painted giraffe is as much for decoration as play. Both adults and children will be charmed by the exotic bird riding on the back of its long-necked friend.
The simple wheeled construction can easily be adapted to make with other animals of your own design.

MATERIALS

¼in birch plywood
8 × 10in

¾in softwood
3 × 3in

³⁄₁₆in dowel
8in

⅛in dowel
2in

¼in dowel
1in

2 eye screws

White wood glue

Toy-safe paints

Varnish

EQUIPMENT

Fretsaw

Tenon saw

Drill and bits
⅛in, ³⁄₁₆in

Sandpaper

Round-nosed pliers

Craft knife

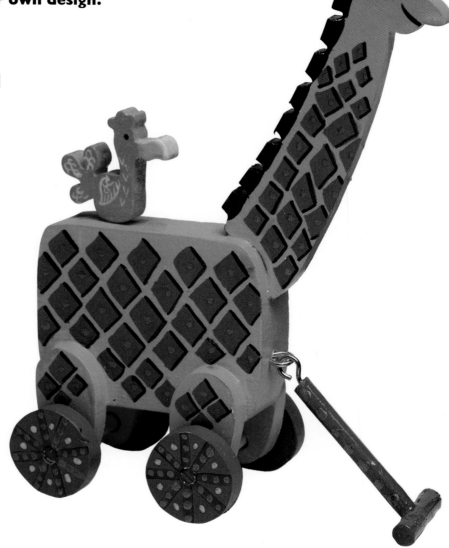

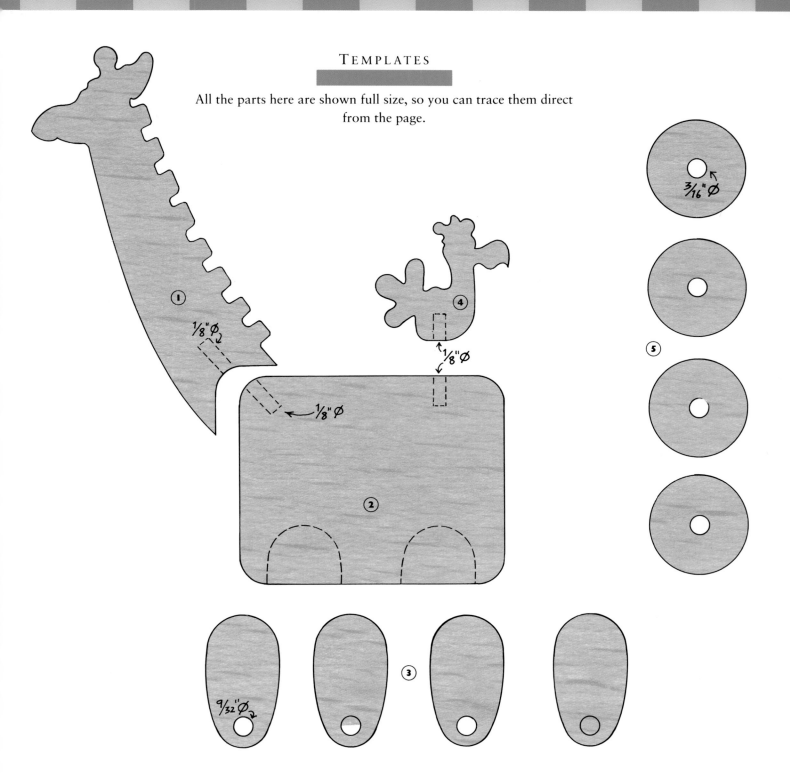

TEMPLATES

All the parts here are shown full size, so you can trace them direct from the page.

① ⅛" Ø₂

④

⅛" Ø

← ⅛" Ø

②

③

⑤ 3/16" Ø

9/32" Ø₂

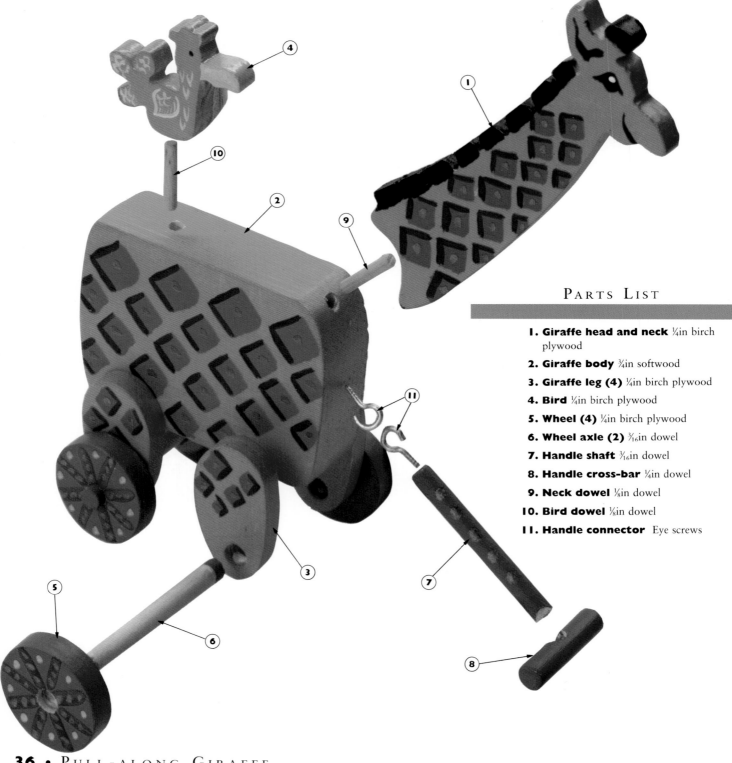

PARTS LIST

1. **Giraffe head and neck** ¼in birch plywood
2. **Giraffe body** ¾in softwood
3. **Giraffe leg (4)** ¼in birch plywood
4. **Bird** ¼in birch plywood
5. **Wheel (4)** ¼in birch plywood
6. **Wheel axle (2)** ³⁄₁₆in dowel
7. **Handle shaft** ³⁄₁₆in dowel
8. **Handle cross-bar** ¼in dowel
9. **Neck dowel** ⅛in dowel
10. **Bird dowel** ⅛in dowel
11. **Handle connector** Eye screws

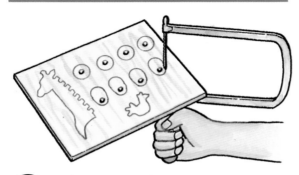

1 Make templates for the parts and transfer them to the type of wood indicated. Drill all marked holes with the appropriate bit and use a coping saw to cut out the plywood parts. Cut two 2-inch lengths of ³⁄₁₆-inch dowel for the axles (6).

2 Hold the head and neck (1) against the softwood block on which you have marked the body in the corner where it will be positioned. Mark the curve on the corner of the body so that when it is cut the two parts will fit snugly. Cut out the body with a fretsaw.

3 Clamp the neck upside down in a vise and drill a hole about ⅜ inch deep with a ⅛-inch bit. Glue a ¾-inch length of ⅛-inch dowel (9) into the hole.

4 Hold the neck against the body in the position marked previously and mark the line of the neck dowel on the body.

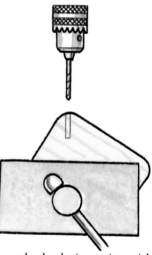

5 Clamp the body in a vise with the marked corner up so that the line of the neck dowel is vertical. Using this line as a guide, drill a ⅛-inch hole in the center of body to a depth of about ⅜ inch. Adjust the position and drill a hole in the center of the giraffe's back to the same depth for the bird dowel (10). Apply glue to the underside of the neck and to the exposed end of the neck dowel and insert into the hole in the body.

6 Apply glue to the inner surface of the upper part of the two front legs. Position them on either side of the body and, before the glue has dried, pass one of the axles (6) through the holes. Adjust the positions of the legs, making sure that the leg holes align. Allow to dry with the axle in place. Repeat for the back legs.

7 Cut a 1-inch length of ¼-inch dowel for the handle crossbar (8). Drill a hole through the center with a ³⁄₁₆-inch bit. Cut a 2½-inch length of ³⁄₁₆-inch dowel for the handle shaft (7) and glue one end of this into the crossbar.

PAINTING AND ASSEMBLY

This is a decorative rather than robust plaything. Don't forget some feathery detail on the bird.

8 Sand all edges smooth and apply two coats of white paint to all the wooden parts. Thread the wheels onto some scrap dowel for ease of handling while painting.

9 Paint the parts as shown. Allow the background orange of the giraffe and the blue of the wheels to dry before painting the patterns. A dot of gold paint at the center of each of the blue diamonds and in the spokes of the wheels creates a jewel-like effect. Don't forget to paint the giraffe's tail black. When the paint is dry, apply a coat of varnish.

10 Insert the axles through the legs. Apply glue inside the holes in the wheels and attach them on the axles.

11 Clamp the bird upside down in a vise and drill a ⅛-inch hole in the center of its body to a depth of ⅜ inch. Glue the bird onto its dowel and into position on the giraffe's back. Leave to dry.

12 Use the pliers to open the loops in the ends of the two eye screws slightly. Screw one into the end of the handle, the other into the giraffe's chest just below the neck. Link the eyes and close to secure.

· WADDLING DUCKS ·

The design of this charming set of waddling barnyard ducks has its origins in Bavaria in southern Germany, and examples of toys of this kind can be seen in the **Nuremberg Toy Museum**. The surprisingly lifelike waddling motion is produced simply by sliding the parallel handles that form the base to which the ducks are attached.

MATERIALS

⅛in birch plywood
10 × 4in

Softwood
2 × 1 × 6in

⅛in birch dowel
3in

⅝in gimp tacks brass
or mild steel
(× 6)

Rapid-drying epoxy
glue

Toy-safe paints

Varnish

White wood glue

EQUIPMENT

Tenon saw

Fretsaw

Drill and bits
¾₄in, ⅛in, ¼in

Mini drill chuck

Needle-nosed pliers

Rasp or coarse
sandpaper

Sandpaper

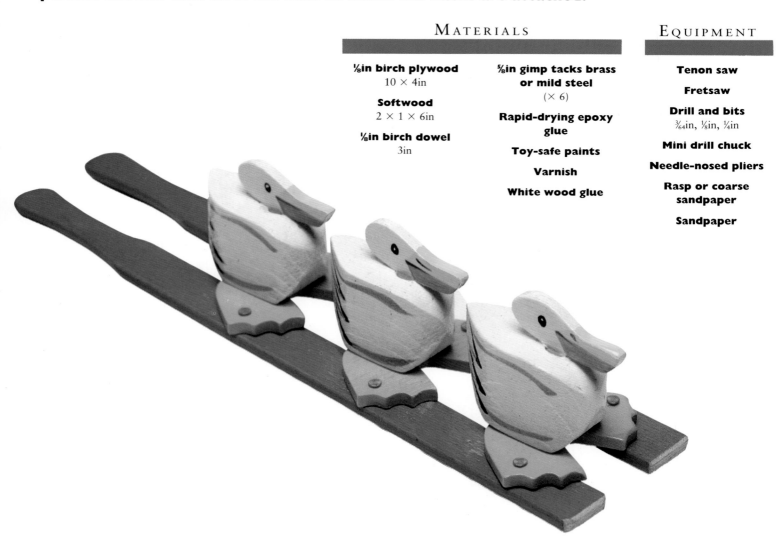

TEMPLATES AND PLANS

The scale here is 75 percent, or 3:4. Use the top elevation as a positional guide.

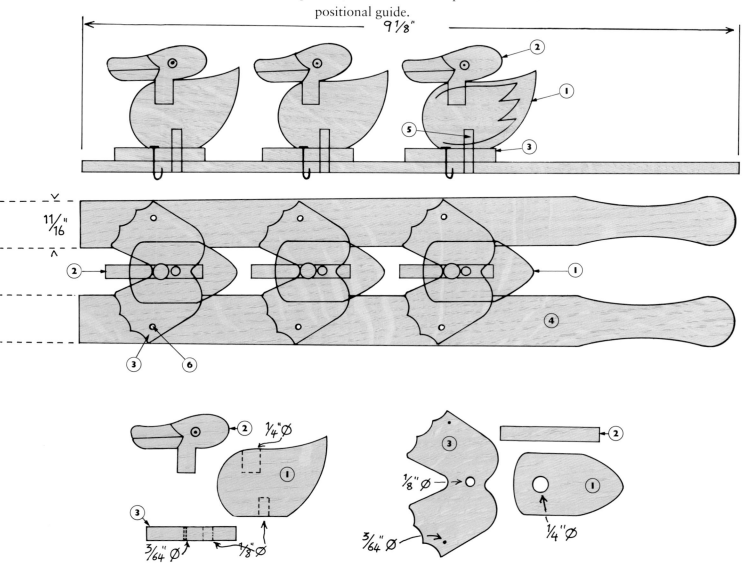

PARTS LIST

1. **Duck body** (3) Softwood
2. **Duck head** (3) ⅛in birch plywood
3. **Duck feet** (3) ⅛in birch plywood
4. **Handles** (2) ⅛in birch plywood
5. **Attaching dowels** (3) ⅛in birch dowel
6. **Pivots** (6) ⅝in gimp tacks

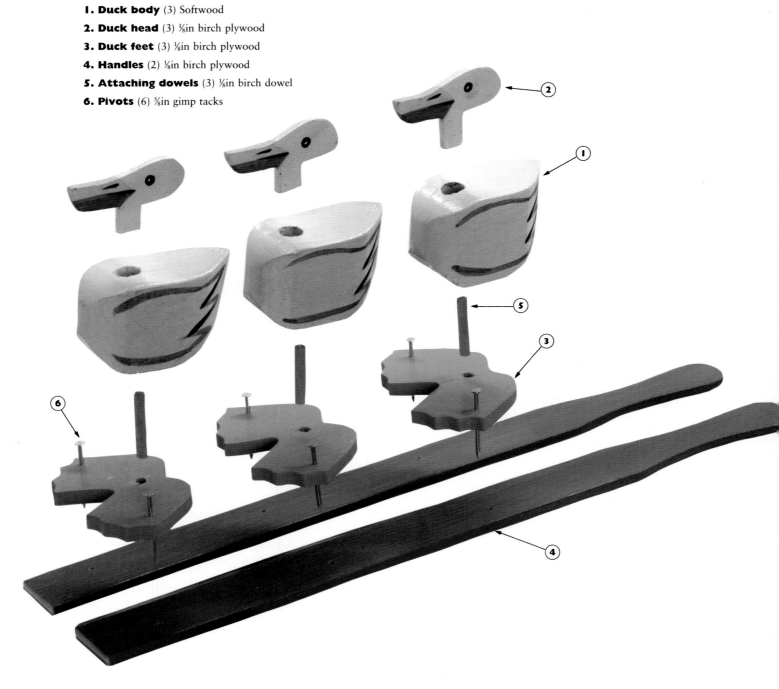

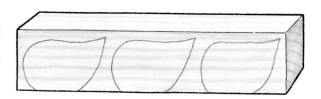

1 Trace three copies of the template for the duck bodies (1) and mark the shapes on the 2-inch side of the softwood.

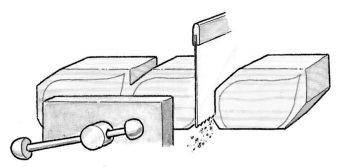

2 Place the wood in a vise and use a tenon saw to separate the body pieces. Do not attempt to shape them yet.

3 Now use a rasp or coarse sandpaper to shape the body profile of each piece, following the lines of the template.

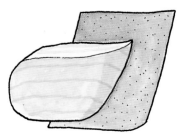

4 Round the front of the body and form the tail into a point. When you are satisfied with the shape, sand the bodies smooth with fine sandpaper.

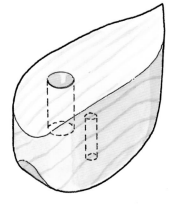

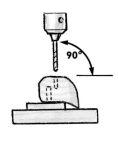

5 Drill holes in each body piece as indicated, using ¼-inch and ⅛-inch bits to a depth of $\frac{5}{16}$ inch. Make sure that the holes are at right angles to the horizontal by placing some scrap wood under the curves of the body as you work.

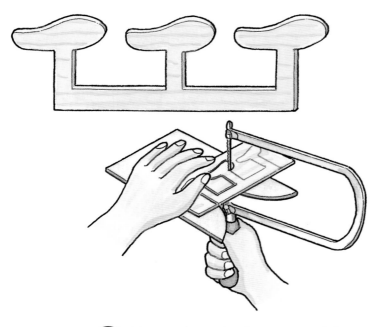

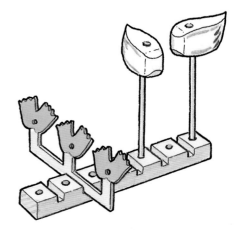

6 Trace and transfer three copies of the head template (2) to the plywood. Place the templates so as to allow for a "sprue" that links the pieces together. Cut out the shapes and sprue, using a fretsaw.

8 Paint all the parts as required, allowing each color to dry before applying the next. Stand the pieces to dry in a rack made from scrap softwood. When you have completed painting, apply two coats of varnish.

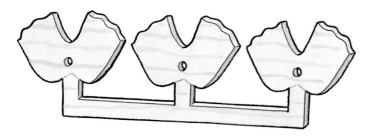

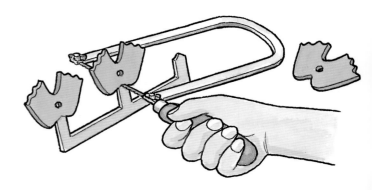

7 Cut out the feet (3) in the same way and drill the holes indicated with a ¼-inch and ³⁄₆₄-inch bit. Cut out the handles (4), allowing about 1 inch extra at the end for holding during painting.

9 Cut the plywood parts from the sprue with a fretsaw and trim the handles. Touch up the paintwork, if necessary.

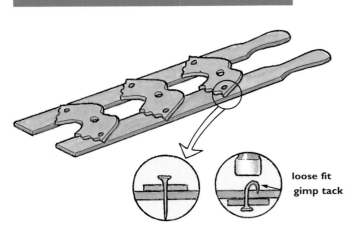

loose fit
gimp tack

10 Position the feet on the handles as shown, and secure with gimp tacks. Hammer these through the small holes in the feet and through the handles so that the ends protrude on the underside of the handles. Bend the ends over with pliers, and gently hammer them into the wood. The nails should be loose enough for the feet to move.

11 Apply glue inside the holes in the top of the body pieces. Position the heads inside the holes, making sure that they are facing forward. Allow to dry.

12 Cut three ⅝-inch lengths of dowel and insert a dowel into the hole in the center of each of the feet. Roughen the underside of the body pieces and the area around the holes in the feet with sandpaper. Apply glue to the underside of the body pieces and position each piece over the dowels on the feet, facing forward. Allow to dry.

· ROLLING RATTLE ·

This decorative and sturdy toy uses very few pieces, and its simple construction makes it an ideal project for a novice wood-worker. Its simplicity and attractive colors will delight a young child, providing hours of amusement.

EQUIPMENT

Fretsaw

Tenon saw

Drill and bit
¼in

Mouth spray airbrush

C-clamps

Sandpaper

Square

Protractor

Cocktail stick

MATERIALS

⅜in birch plywood
3⁵⁄₁₆ × 6⅝in

¼in birch dowel
(13in)

**¾in wooden beads
with ⁹⁄₃₂in holes**
(× 4)

Thin posterboard
3½ × 3½in

1¼in scrap wood
1¾ × 1½in

⅞in scrap softwood
4¾ × 5½in

Paint primer

Toy-safe paints

Varnish

White wood glue

Double-sided tape

TEMPLATES AND PLANS

All the templates are shown full size (1:1), except for the spiral spraying guide, which is 66:7 percent (2:3).

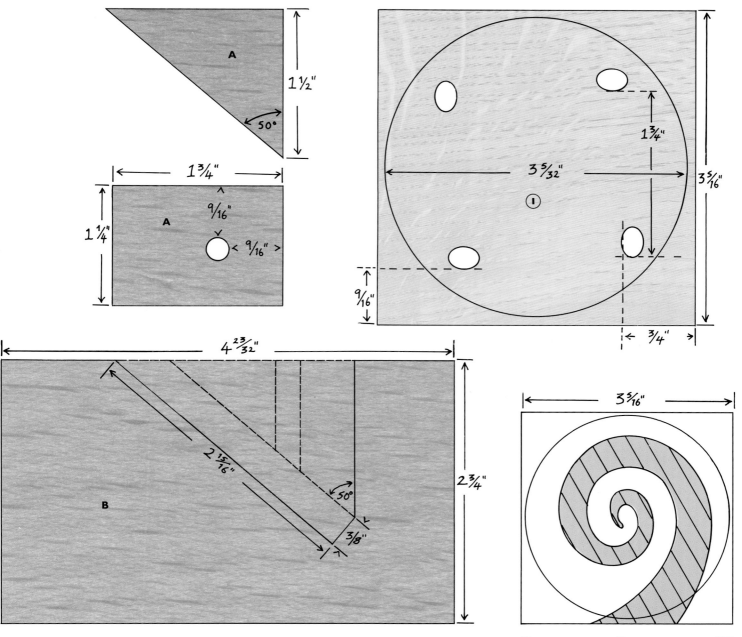

1. Bases (2) Birch plywood

2. Struts (4) Birch dowel

3. Rattles (4) Wooden beads

MAKING THE PARTS

1 Apply two coats of varnish to the dowel. When dry, cut into four $3\frac{1}{16}$-inch lengths and rub the last $\frac{1}{4}$ inch at each end with sandpaper. Cut the plywood into two $3\frac{5}{16}$-inch squares.

2 To make the drilling jig, cut the $\frac{7}{8}$-inch scrap wood in half to give pieces B and C measuring $2\frac{3}{4} \times 4\frac{3}{4}$ inches. Using the template as a guide, cut the wedge out of piece B.

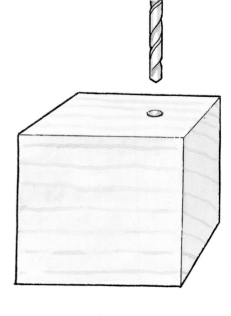

3 Drill a vertical hole with a $\frac{1}{4}$-inch bit through the $1\frac{1}{4}$-inch scrap wood as shown.

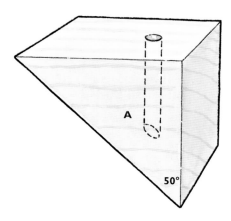

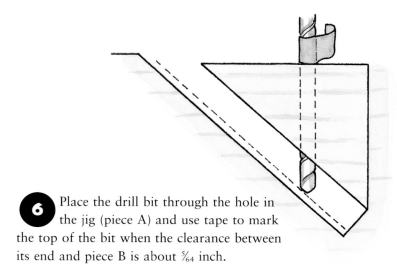

4 Then cut the piece in half diagonally with a tenon saw to form a wedge shape (piece A).

6 Place the drill bit through the hole in the jig (piece A) and use tape to mark the top of the bit when the clearance between its end and piece B is about $\frac{5}{64}$ inch.

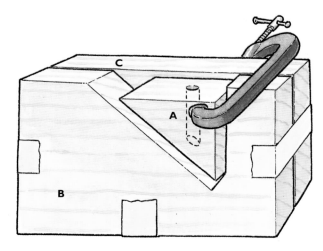

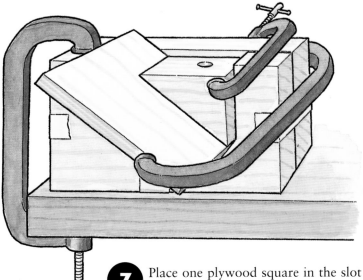

5 Glue pieces B and C together, then attach piece A to B and C with masking tape, as shown. Hold this firm with a small C-clamp.

7 Place one plywood square in the slot and clamp firmly in position. Drill through the hole until the bit reaches the mark. Turn the square and repeat until you have drilled a hole in each corner. Drill the second square in the same way.

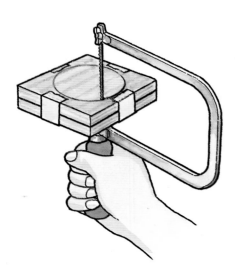

8 Tape the squares together and, using template D or a compass, draw and cut out a 3⅛-inch diameter circle. Separate the pieces (1) and smooth the edges.

9 Paint the rim of each disk with two coats of primer and, when dry, apply two coats of blue paint, sanding between coats. Allow to dry.

10 Cut two templates (E) from posterboard. Attach these to the (undrilled) faces of the disks with thin strips of double-sided tape. Lightly spray them with diluted red paint. When dry, apply a further light coat, if needed.

11 Thread two beads onto a piece of scrap dowel and spray one side with red paint. Wash the airbrush. Turn the beads and spray the other side with diluted blue paint. Spray the remaining two beads blue on one side and green on the other. When the paint is dry, varnish all parts. Avoid getting varnish in the holes. Allow to dry.

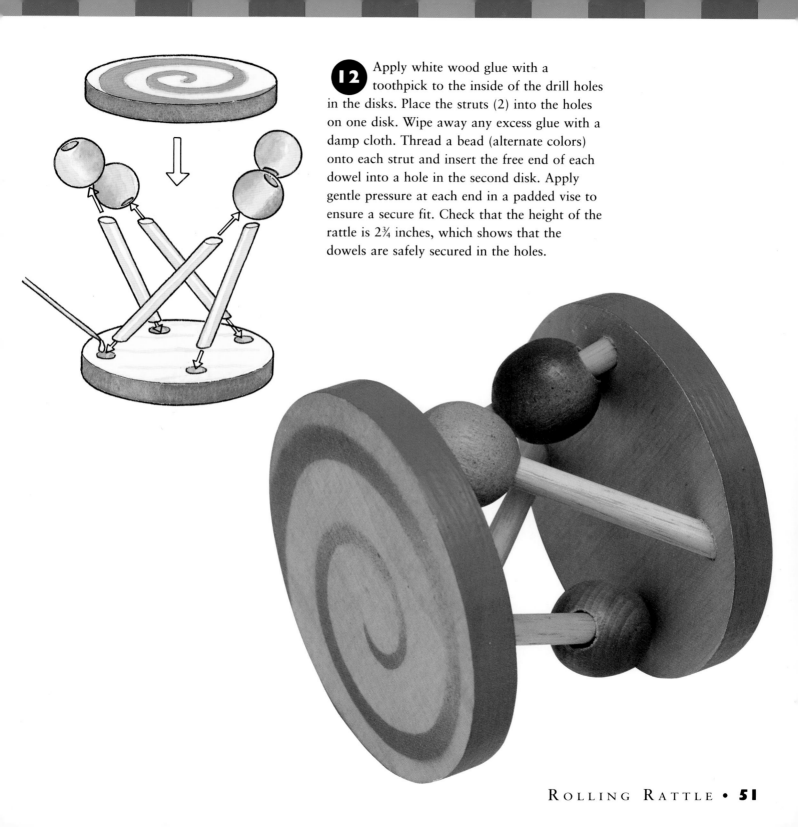

12 Apply white wood glue with a toothpick to the inside of the drill holes in the disks. Place the struts (2) into the holes on one disk. Wipe away any excess glue with a damp cloth. Thread a bead (alternate colors) onto each strut and insert the free end of each dowel into a hole in the second disk. Apply gentle pressure at each end in a padded vise to ensure a secure fit. Check that the height of the rattle is 2¾ inches, which shows that the dowels are safely secured in the holes.

· MONSTER ROCKET ·

This easily made toy "magically" transforms from a friendly monster to a space-age rocket. Attractively designed in bright colors, it provides lots of fun for young children, who will happily occupy themselves pulling out the different elements to create the plaything of their choice.

MATERIALS

⅛in birch plywood
24 × 6½in

⅛in dowel
7½in

¾₄in metal washers
with ⅛in holes

White wood glue

Masking tape

Double-sided tape

Toy-safe dyes

Varnish

EQUIPMENT

Fretsaw

Drill and bits
1⁄16in, 5⁄32in

Sandpaper

Round file (optional)

TEMPLATES AND PLANS

These templates are at 50 percent, or 1:2. Use the cutting guide to minimize wastage.

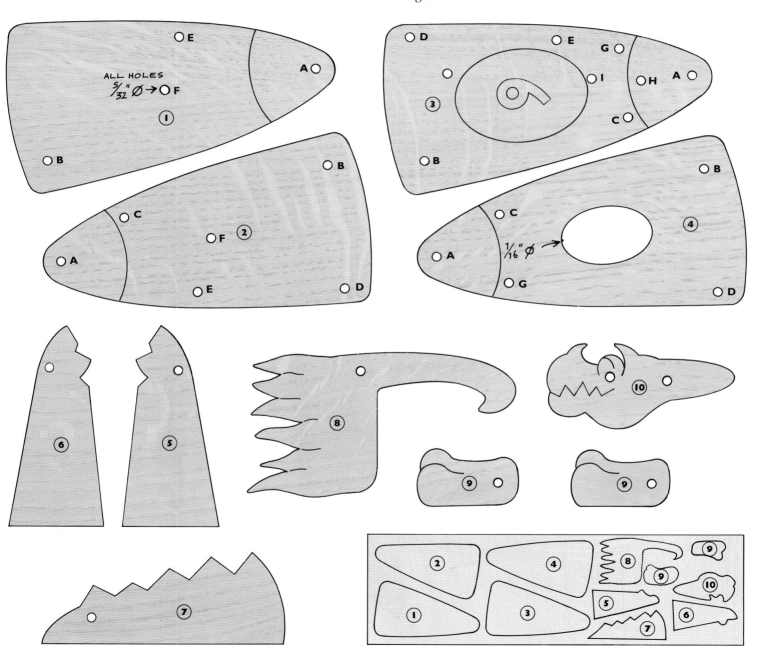

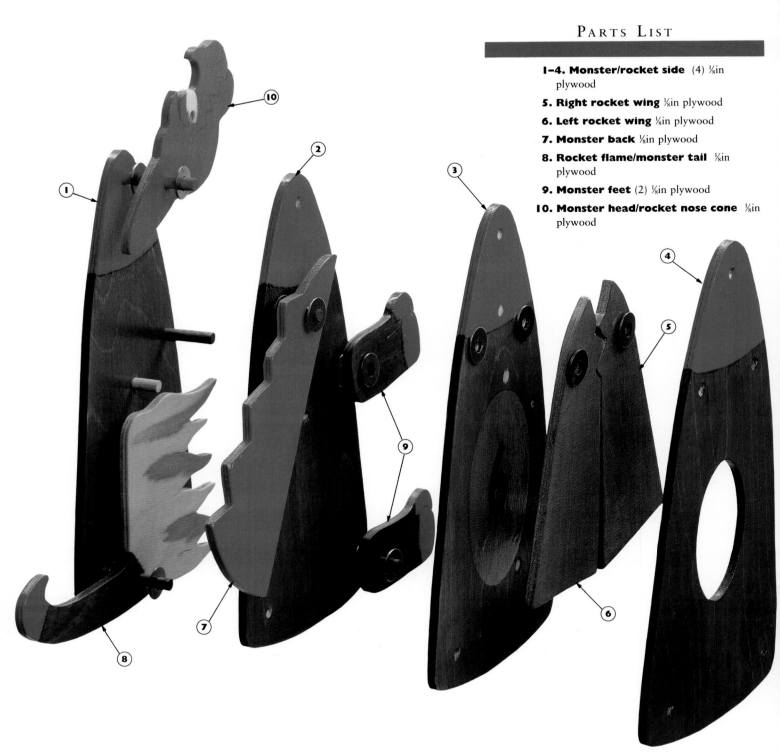

PARTS LIST

1–4. Monster/rocket side (4) ⅛in plywood

5. Right rocket wing ⅛in plywood

6. Left rocket wing ⅛in plywood

7. Monster back ⅛in plywood

8. Rocket flame/monster tail ⅛in plywood

9. Monster feet (2) ⅛in plywood

10. Monster head/rocket nose cone ⅛in plywood

1 Cut the dowel to the following lengths: three 5/16-inch pieces; two ½-inch pieces; three ⅞-inch pieces; two 1¾16-inch pieces.

2 Trace the templates and use double-sided tape to attach them to the plywood. Use a fretsaw to cut between the shapes.

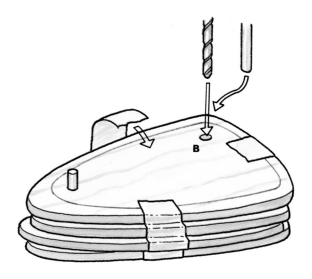

4 With piece no. 1 on top, drill hole B through all four pieces, using the same bit. Insert the other 1¾16-inch length of dowel into this hole.

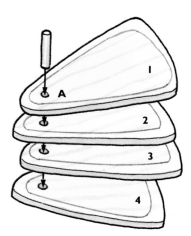

3 Drill hole A through the template on each body piece (1, 2, 3 and 4) using a 5/32-inch bit. Sandwich all four pieces together in that order and insert a 1¾16-inch length of dowel through the hole to line up the pieces. Secure in position with masking tape.

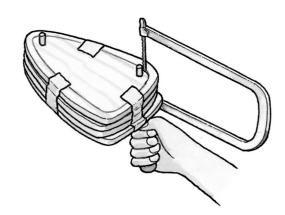

5 Using a fretsaw with a medium blade, cut out the body shape following the template for piece no. 1. Separate the pieces.

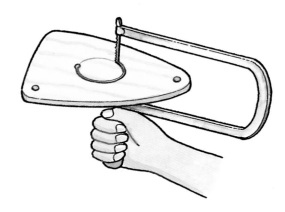

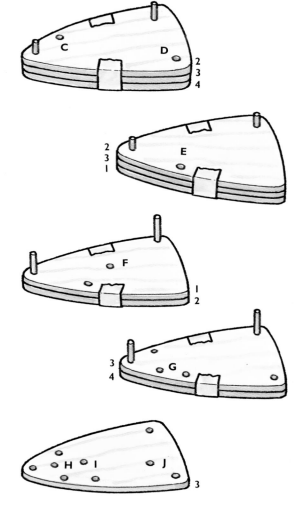

6 Cut out the center of piece no. 4 by drilling a ¹⁄₁₆-inch hole and feeding the fretsaw blade through (see Basic Techniques).

7 Insert the dowels through holes A and B in pieces 1, 2, and 3 to ensure correct alignment. Sand the dowels to ease the fit, if necessary. Tape the pieces together and drill holes C and D through all three pieces with a ⁵⁄₃₂-inch bit. Remove piece no. 4 and replace with no. 1. Secure with tape and drill hole E. Continue drilling the holes in sequence through the different combinations of body pieces as shown. Remove templates.

8 Arrange the body pieces and insert the dowels into the holes, as shown, flush to the underside of each piece. Apply glue to the rim of the dowel ends to secure. Wipe away any excess glue with a damp cloth.

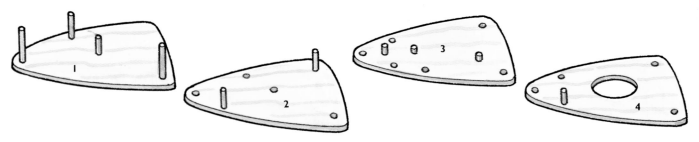

9 Drill the holes marked in pieces 5 to 10 with a 5/32-inch bit. If the holes in pieces 5 and 6 are not positioned precisely as on the templates, reposition the templates so that the holes marked are exactly over the drilled holes. Cut out the pieces with a fretsaw.

10 Lightly sand all pieces. Paint both sides of all pieces and any dowel ends that will show in the colors indicated. Paint any number of your choice, within an oval on the reverse side of piece 3. Varnish all invisible parts if required, except the stems of the dowels.

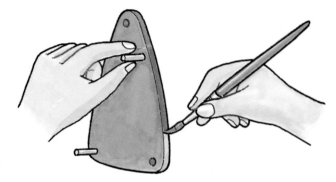

11 When dry, assemble the pieces, with washers placed between the moving parts. When you have checked that all the parts move in and out of the body freely, dismantle. Reassemble in stages as illustrated, putting a small dab of glue on the rims of the dowel ends as you work. Make sure that none of the dowels protrude through the surface.

·FLYING SWAN·

Nothing can beat the exhilarating sight of a flock of swans in full flight. Recreate this experience in your own home with this graceful bird that rhythmically flaps its wings when hung from the ceiling. This is a superb toy for both adults and children that is not hard to make, either from the woodworking point of view, or that of the decoration.

MATERIALS

¼in birch plywood
24 × 24in

⅝in dowel
18in

Large wooden bead
with ⅜in hole

Brass curtain ring

String
30in

Nylon fishing line
10ft

Toy-safe paints

White wood glue

Double-sided tape

EQUIPMENT

Fretsaw

Drill and bits
⁵⁄₆₄in, ⁵⁄₃₂in

Sandpaper

Scissors

TEMPLATES

These templates are shown at 30 percent, or 3:10. A cutting guide is also shown.

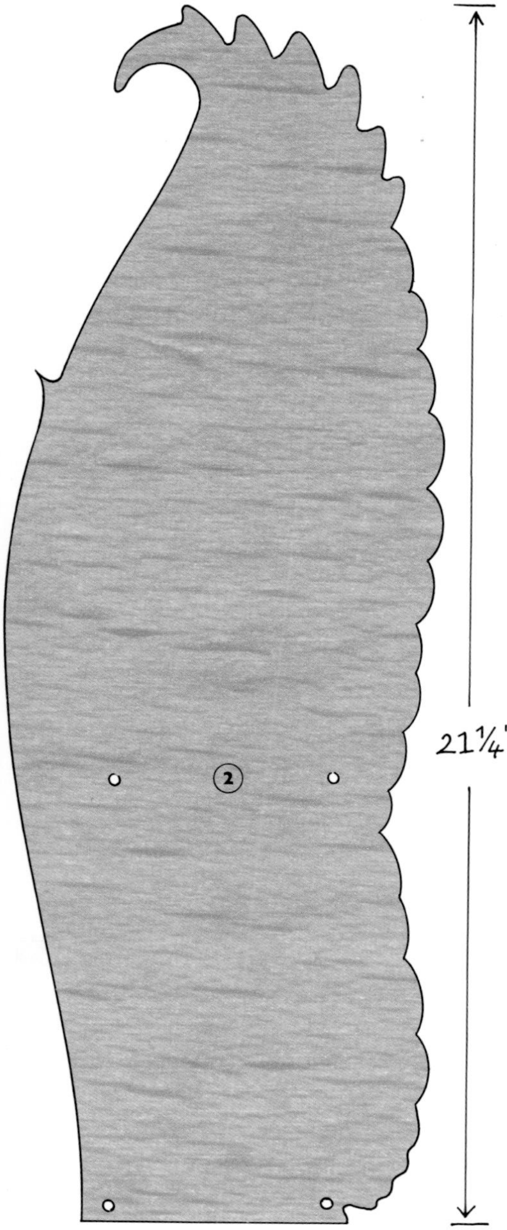

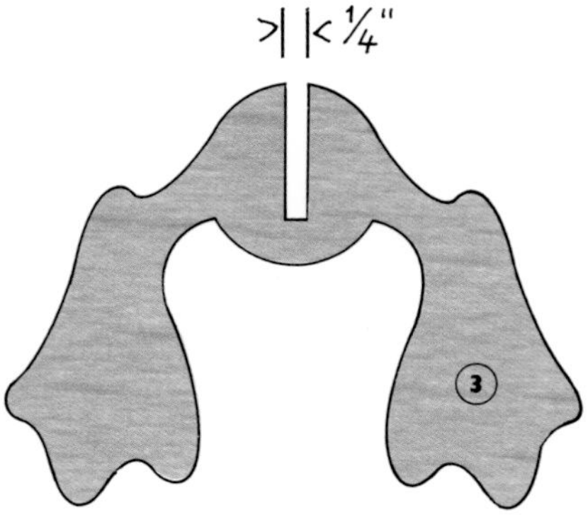

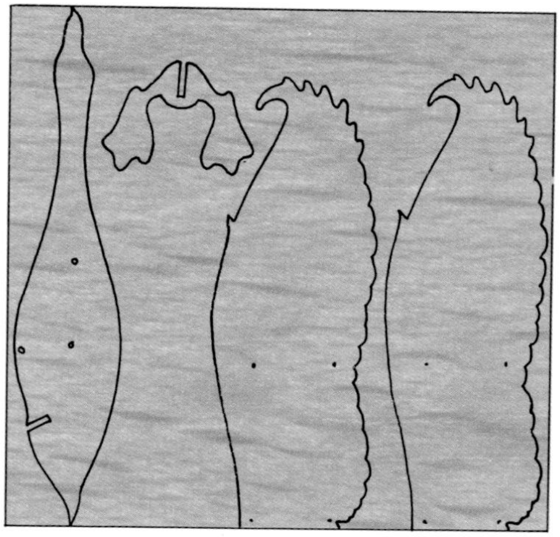

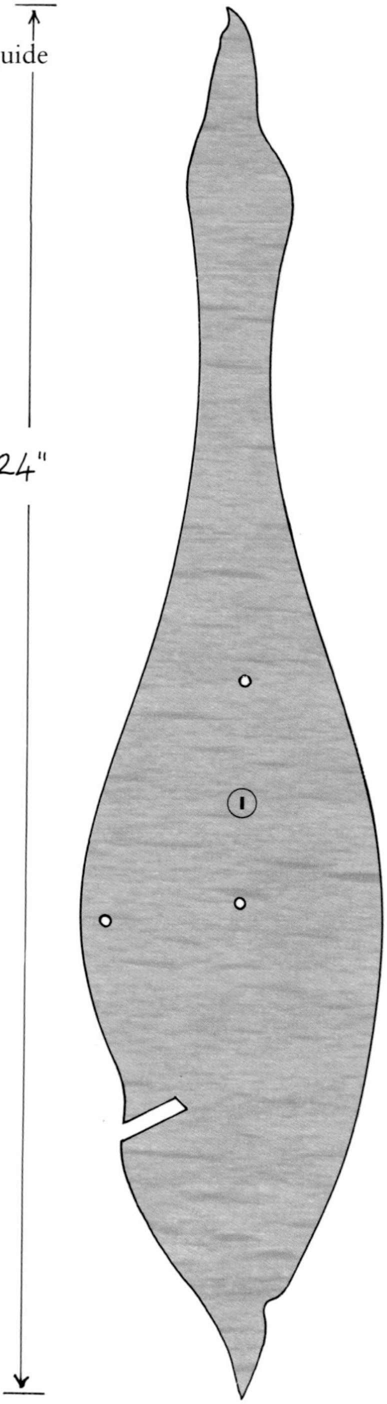

>| |< ¼"

24"

21¼"

② ① ③

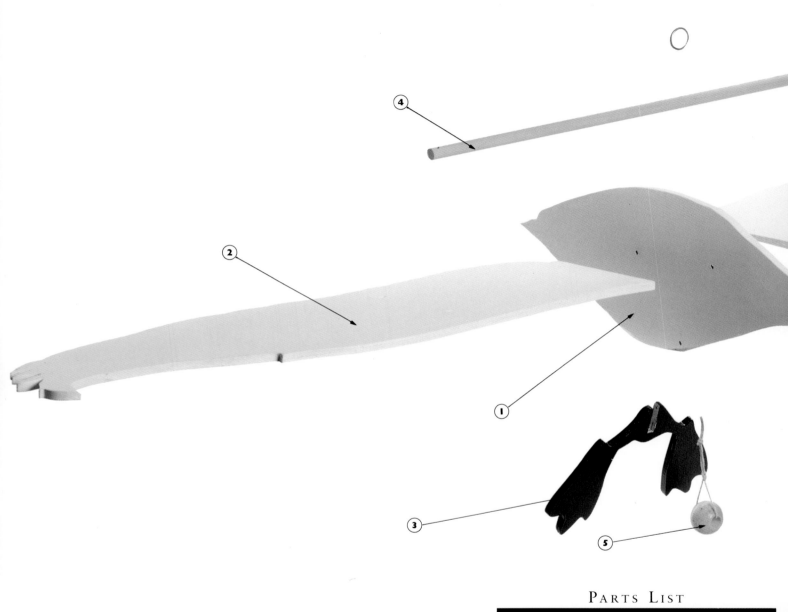

PARTS LIST

1. Body ¼in birch plywood

2. Wing (2) ¼in birch plywood

3. Feet ¼in birch plywood

4. Dowel ⅛in dowel

5. Pulling bead Wooden bead

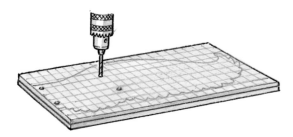

1 Make templates for the body (1), one wing (2), and feet (3) by scaling up the diagrams (see Basic Techniques). Mark the body piece on the plywood and drill the holes specified with a ⁵⁄₆₄-inch bit. Cut out the shape with a fretsaw.

2 Cut the remaining plywood so that you have two pieces large enough for the wing template. Attach the two pieces together with double-sided tape and mark the wing on the upper surface. Drill the specified holes through both layers with a ⁵⁄₆₄-inch bit, and cut out the wing shape with a fretsaw.

3 Mark the feet on a single sheet of the remaining plywood and cut out with a fretsaw. Sand all parts to a smooth finish.

PAINTING THE PARTS

4 Apply two coats of white paint to all the plywood parts. Paint the body and wings with a white top coat and paint the feet black. When the white paint is dry, add the details of the eyes and beak on both sides of the head.

ASSEMBLY

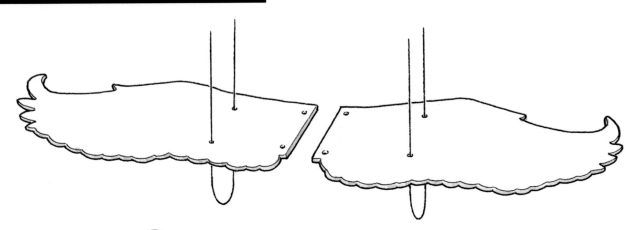

5 Cut two 40-inch lengths of nylon fishing line and thread them through the central holes in the wings, as shown.

6 Cut two more pieces of nylon, each about 6 inches long and tie them around the holes on the inner edge of one wing, leaving loose ends of approximately equal length.

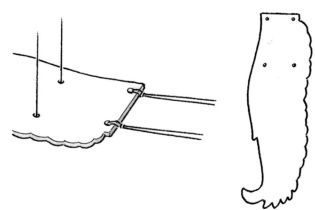

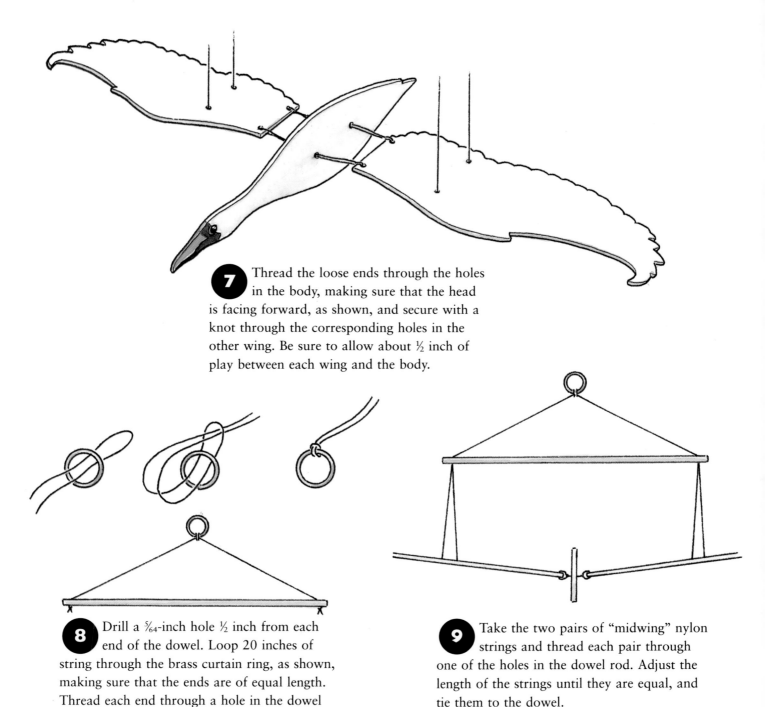

7 Thread the loose ends through the holes in the body, making sure that the head is facing forward, as shown, and secure with a knot through the corresponding holes in the other wing. Be sure to allow about ½ inch of play between each wing and the body.

8 Drill a ⁵⁄₆₄-inch hole ½ inch from each end of the dowel. Loop 20 inches of string through the brass curtain ring, as shown, making sure that the ends are of equal length. Thread each end through a hole in the dowel rod, and tie a knot to secure.

9 Take the two pairs of "midwing" nylon strings and thread each pair through one of the holes in the dowel rod. Adjust the length of the strings until they are equal, and tie them to the dowel.

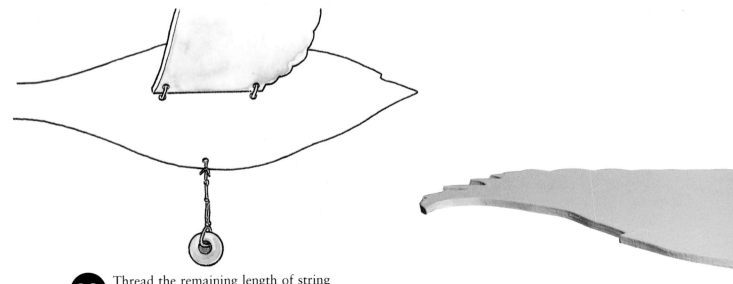

10 Thread the remaining length of string through the wooden bead. Tie the two ends together several times as shown and tie to the hole in the underside of the body.

11 Slot the feet onto the body in the position indicated on the template. Glue to secure, if necessary. Suspend the whole assembly from the curtain ring, hanging perhaps from a hook in the ceiling. Gently pull and release the bead to start the wings flapping.

· ROOSTER ROLLER ·

As you roll the wheels of this colorful comic rooster, the wings flap alternately and the clicking of the cams makes a soft clucking noise. Very simple to make, this toy will delight any young child.

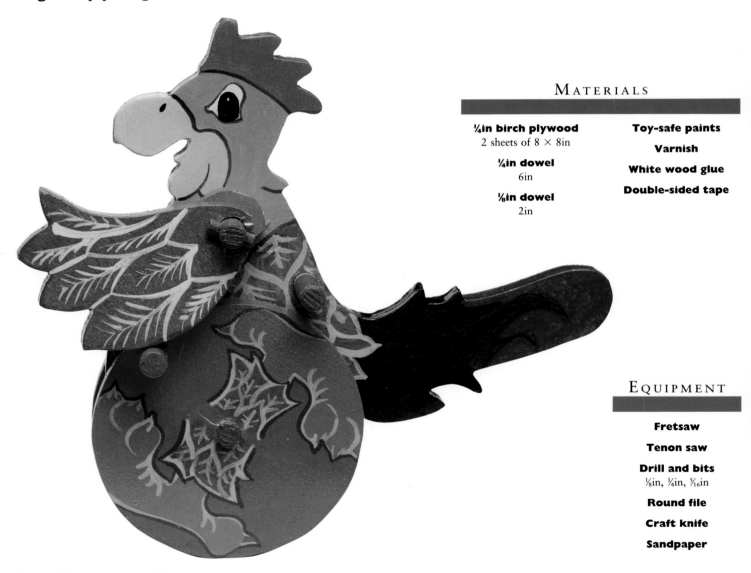

MATERIALS

¼in birch plywood
2 sheets of 8 × 8in

¼in dowel
6in

⅛in dowel
2in

Toy-safe paints

Varnish

White wood glue

Double-sided tape

EQUIPMENT

Fretsaw

Tenon saw

Drill and bits
⅛in, ¼in, ⁵⁄₁₆in

Round file

Craft knife

Sandpaper

Templates

All parts here are full size, so you can trace them straight from the page.

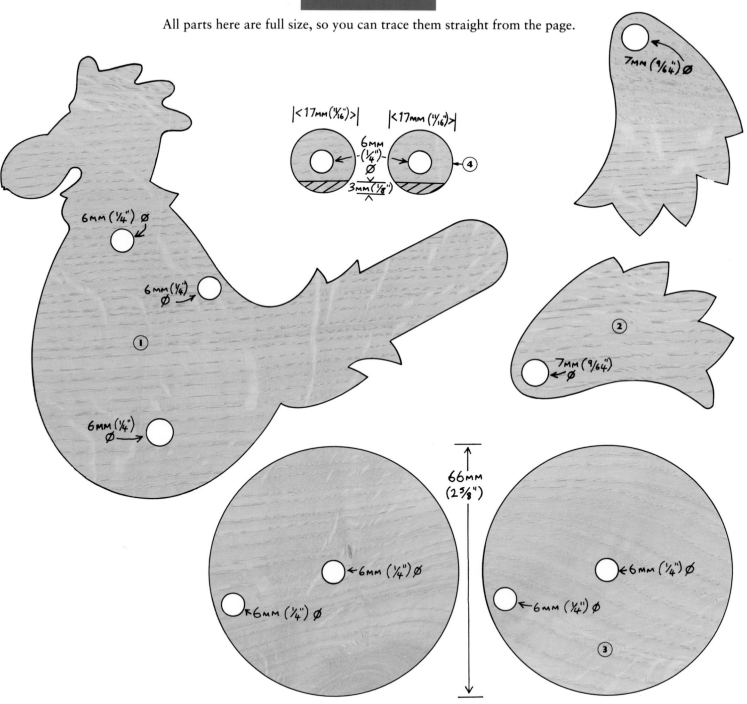

|<17mm (¹¹/₁₆")>| |<17mm (¹¹/₁₆")>|

6mm
(¹/₄")
Ø

3mm (¹/₈")

④

7mm (⁹/₆₄") Ø

6mm (¹/₄") Ø

6mm (¹/₄")
Ø

①

②

7mm (⁹/₆₄")
Ø

6mm (¹/₄")
Ø

66mm
(2⅝")

←6mm (¹/₄") Ø

←6mm (¹/₄") Ø

←6mm (¹/₄") Ø

←6mm (¹/₄") Ø

③

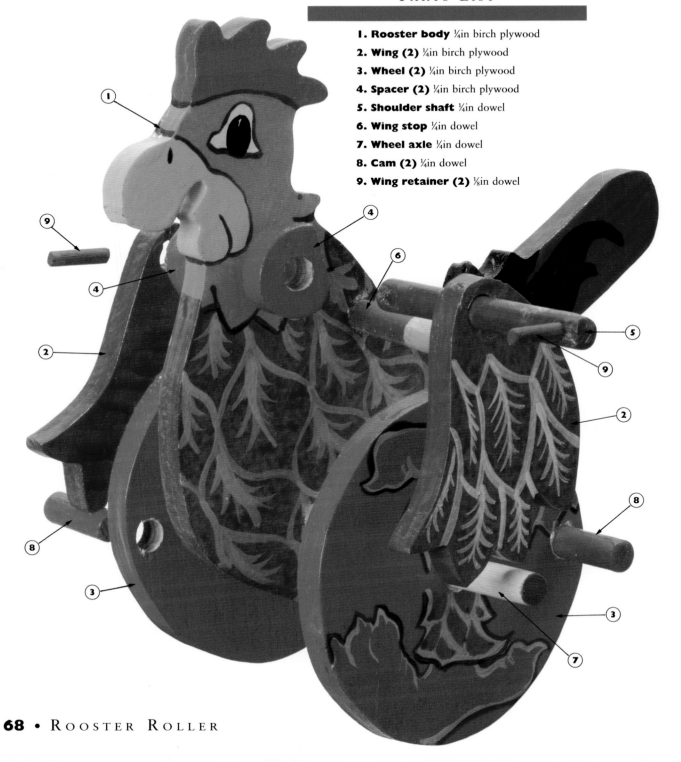

Parts List

1. **Rooster body** ¼in birch plywood
2. **Wing (2)** ¼in birch plywood
3. **Wheel (2)** ¼in birch plywood
4. **Spacer (2)** ⅛in birch plywood
5. **Shoulder shaft** ¼in dowel
6. **Wing stop** ¼in dowel
7. **Wheel axle** ¼in dowel
8. **Cam (2)** ¼in dowel
9. **Wing retainer (2)** ⅛in dowel

MAKING THE PARTS

1 Make templates of the parts from the diagrams. Attach the two sheets of ¼-inch birch plywood together with double-sided tape. Transfer the designs onto the plywood.

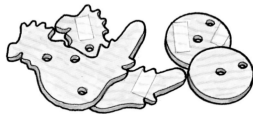

2 Drill all marked holes with the size of bit specified, and cut out the shapes with a fretsaw. Separate the two layers of plywood and sand the parts smooth with fine sandpaper. Discard the spare rooster body (1) or use as scrap.

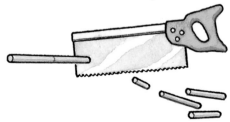

3 Measure and cut the ¼-inch dowel into the following lengths: 1¾ inches (wing stop – 6); 2¾ inches (shoulder shaft – 5); 1 inch (wheel axle – 7); 2 × ¾ inch (cams – 8). Cut the ⅛-inch dowel into two lengths of ½ inch for the wing retainers (9). Smooth the ends of each dowel with fine sandpaper.

4 Drill a ⅛-inch hole through the shoulder shaft dowel (5), ³⁄₁₆ inch from each end.

PAINTING THE PARTS

5 Apply two coats of white paint to all parts and allow to dry. Following the illustrations, lightly draw in the details of the painted decoration, using a pencil. Paint the parts in the colors shown, using a fine synthetic brush for the details.

6 Paint the head as follows: yellow beak; red comb; white outer eye; black inner eye; orange head and neck. When dry, outline in dark brown.

7 Stipple light brown on the body to give a feathery effect by dabbing the wet paint with a brush. When dry, paint feathers in yellow. Use light and dark green with curved strokes to suggest long tail feathers.

8 The wheels are bright red with legs and feet painted over in yellow. Be sure to paint the feet as shown so that the rooster will appear to "walk" when the wheels turn.

9 Paint the inside surfaces of the wings the same brown as the body. For the outside surfaces, mix a little red with the brown. Stipple this in the same way as for the body. When dry, use white paint for the feather pattern, as shown.

10 Paint the handle (tip of tail) dark brown. When dry, apply two coats of varnish to all parts except dowels.

11 Apply glue inside the outer holes in each wheel and insert the cams (8). Apply glue inside the upper holes in the body and insert the wing stop (6) and shoulder shaft (5), ensuring that the ends of each dowel protrude equally on each side.

12 Slide the spacers (4) over each end of the shoulder shaft. They should be a tight fit and lie against the body, with the rounded sides up.

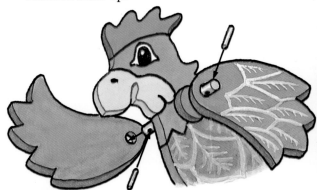

13 Position the wings over the spacers so that they swing freely on the shaft. Enlarge the holes with a round file if necessary. Apply a little glue inside the holes in the ends of the shaft and insert the wing retainers (9).

14 Insert the wheel axle into the lower hole in the body and check that it moves freely. Glue the wheel axle into the central hole in one of the wheels on the opposite side from the cam. With the axle in position, glue the other wheel onto the free end so that the cams are at 180° to each other. Paint visible areas of the dowels.

· Wiggling Water Monster ·

In contrast to the terrifying creatures from the deep who, according to the ancient sea myths, attacked sailors and their boats, this spectacular water monster, with its friendly expression and lively colors, is a most unfrightening play companion. Mount the base on the wall and simply push the dowel rod to see this cheerful creature wiggle its way through the waves.

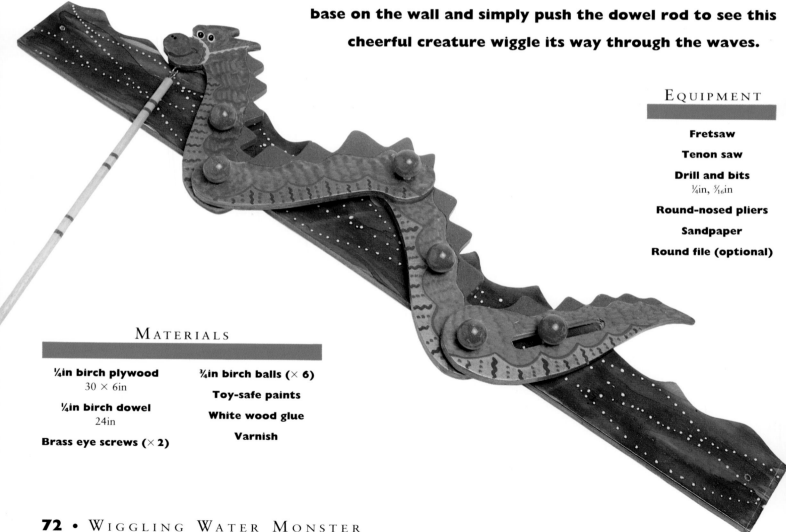

Equipment

Fretsaw

Tenon saw

Drill and bits
¼in, ⁵⁄₁₆in

Round-nosed pliers

Sandpaper

Round file (optional)

Materials

¼in birch plywood
30 × 6in

¼in birch dowel
24in

Brass eye screws (× 2)

¾in birch balls (× 6)

Toy-safe paints

White wood glue

Varnish

TEMPLATES

Parts 1 to 4 are shown at 50 percent, or 1:2, part 5 is at
30 percent, or 3:10.

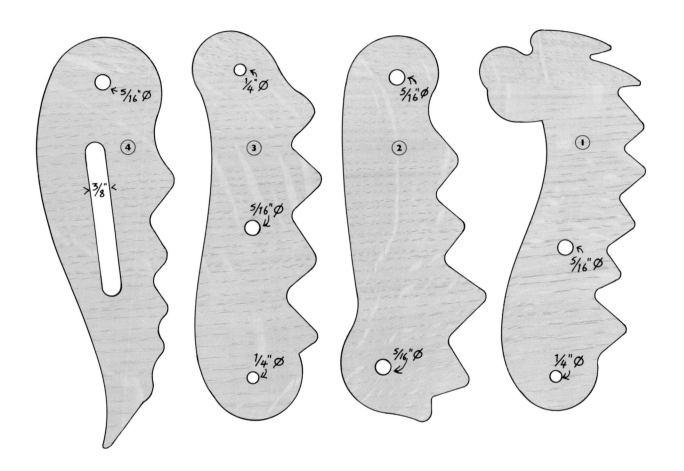

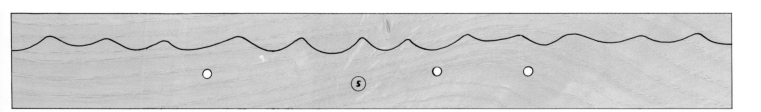

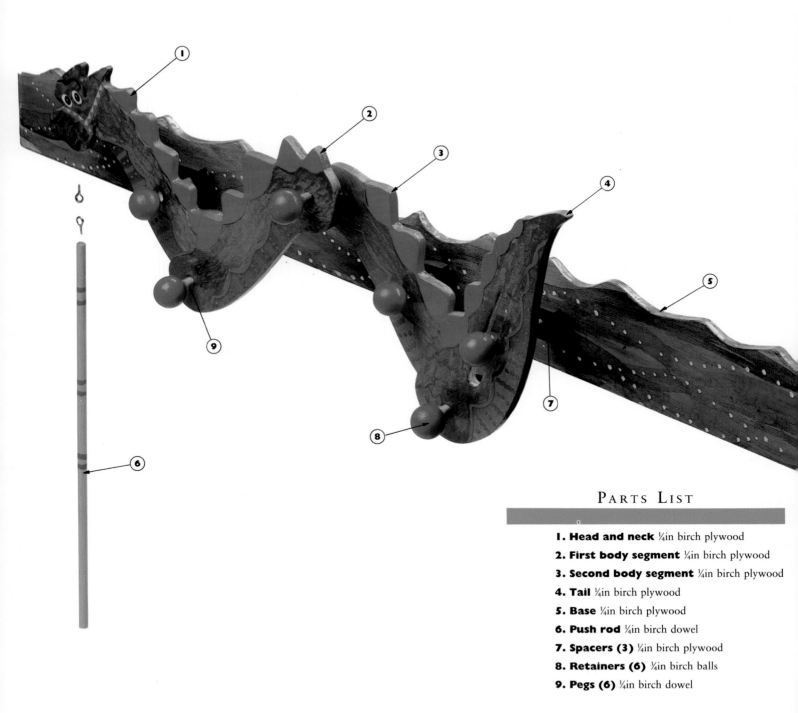

Parts List

1. **Head and neck** ¼in birch plywood
2. **First body segment** ¼in birch plywood
3. **Second body segment** ¼in birch plywood
4. **Tail** ¼in birch plywood
5. **Base** ¼in birch plywood
6. **Push rod** ¼in birch dowel
7. **Spacers (3)** ¼in birch plywood
8. **Retainers (6)** ¾in birch balls
9. **Pegs (6)** ¼in birch dowel

Making the Parts

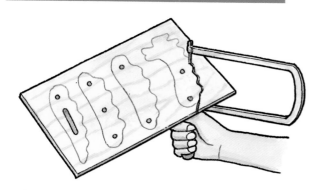

1 Make templates from the diagrams and transfer the shapes onto the ¼-inch birch plywood. Mark and drill the holes with a ⁵⁄₁₆-inch or ¼-inch bit, as specified. Cut out the slot in the tail (see Basic Techniques). Cut out all the pieces with a fretsaw and sand to a smooth finish.

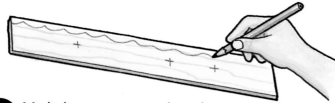

2 Mark the wave pattern along the top edge of a 3 × 24-inch piece of ¼-inch birch plywood, as shown. Drill the holes with a ¼-inch bit and cut out the wave pattern with a fretsaw.

3 Mark out three ¾-inch squares on a piece of ¼-inch birch plywood for the spacers (7) and drill a ⁵⁄₁₆-inch hole through the center of each. Cut out the squares with a tenon saw.

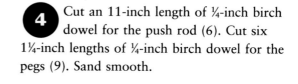

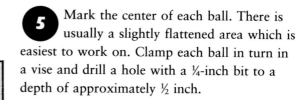

4 Cut an 11-inch length of ¼-inch birch dowel for the push rod (6). Cut six 1¼-inch lengths of ¼-inch birch dowel for the pegs (9). Sand smooth.

5 Mark the center of each ball. There is usually a slightly flattened area which is easiest to work on. Clamp each ball in turn in a vise and drill a hole with a ¼-inch bit to a depth of approximately ½ inch.

6 Check the fit of all pieces. The short pegs should fit tightly into the holes in the base, the spacers, and the balls, but should move freely in the holes and the slot in the monster parts. If necessary, enlarge the holes with a round file.

Painting the Pieces

Make your monster as bright and cheerful as you can, not forgetting a happy smiling face.

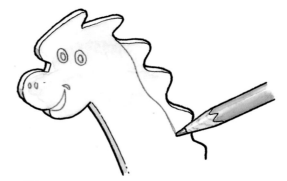

7 Apply two coats of white paint to all pieces and leave to dry. Lightly draw the features and body markings of the monster on the upper surface of the head, body, and tail pieces (1–4), copying the photographs.

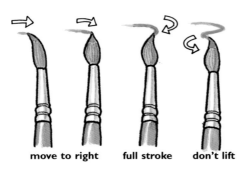

move to right   full stroke   don't lift

8 Thin some green metallic (pearlescent) paint with water and apply to all parts of the monster, except those areas reserved for decoration. Before the paint is dry, wiggle a medium synthetic brush in a rhythmic pattern across the painted surface to create an impression of scales. When the green paint is dry, paint the rest of the markings on the monster, as shown.

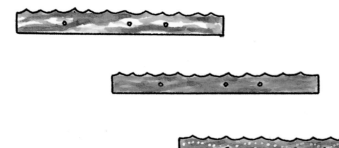

9 Paint the base in shades of diluted blues and greens to suggest waves. Don't cover the whole surface with each color, but leave different areas unpainted with each color to allow different mixes to show through. Allow to dry between coats. When dry, apply white dots of "surf" in wave shapes. Decorate the push rod with bands of red. When all paint is dry, varnish all painted surfaces.

ASSEMBLING THE PIECES

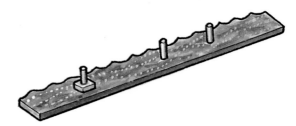

10 Glue three pegs into the holes in the base so that they are flush with the underside. Glue a spacer firmly to the base over each of the pegs.

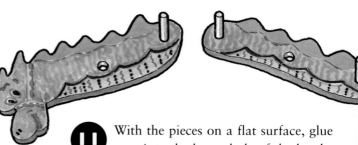

11 With the pieces on a flat surface, glue pegs into the lower hole of the head and neck (1) and into the two outer holes of the second body segment (3) so that they are flush to the underside.

12 Place the free hole in the head and neck over the left-hand peg in the base and the free hole in the second body segment over the middle hole in the base.

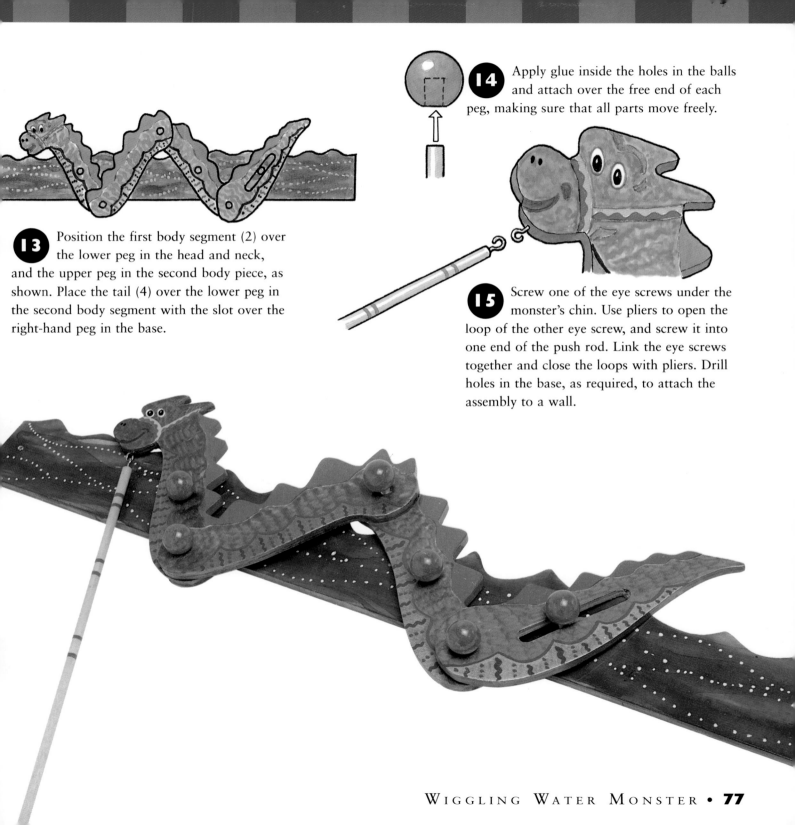

14 Apply glue inside the holes in the balls and attach over the free end of each peg, making sure that all parts move freely.

13 Position the first body segment (2) over the lower peg in the head and neck, and the upper peg in the second body piece, as shown. Place the tail (4) over the lower peg in the second body segment with the slot over the right-hand peg in the base.

15 Screw one of the eye screws under the monster's chin. Use pliers to open the loop of the other eye screw, and screw it into one end of the push rod. Link the eye screws together and close the loops with pliers. Drill holes in the base, as required, to attach the assembly to a wall.

· PECKING HEN ·

This is a simplified version of a toy that is familiar to many of us. The more complicated designs have perhaps five or six birds pecking in turn, and the movement is produced by a swinging wooden ball that raises and lowers the hens' heads. In woodworking terms, this is a very easy project, whose appeal is enhanced by the decoration.

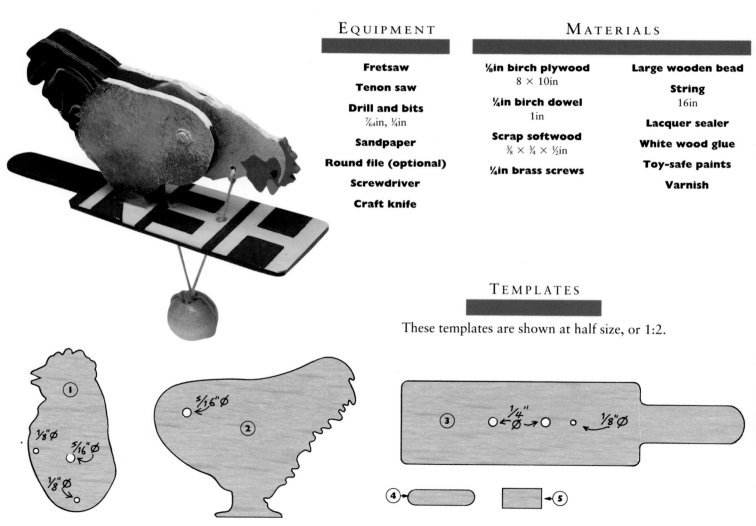

EQUIPMENT

Fretsaw

Tenon saw

Drill and bits
⁷⁄₆₄in, ¼in

Sandpaper

Round file (optional)

Screwdriver

Craft knife

MATERIALS

⅛in birch plywood
8 × 10in

¼in birch dowel
1in

Scrap softwood
⅜ × ¾ × ½in

¼in brass screws

Large wooden bead

String
16in

Lacquer sealer

White wood glue

Toy-safe paints

Varnish

TEMPLATES

These templates are shown at half size, or 1:2.

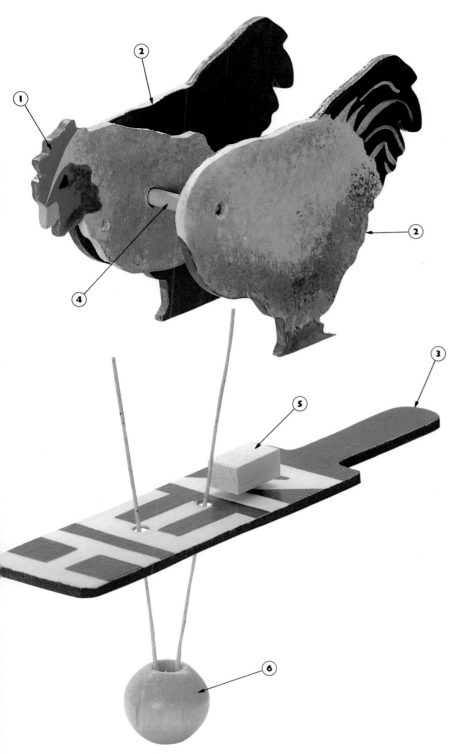

1. **Head and neck** ⅛in birch plywood
2. **Body (2)** ⅛in birch plywood
3. **Base** ⅛in birch plywood
4. **Neck pivot** ¼in dowel
5. **Spacer** Scrap softwood
6. **Pendulum** Wooden bead

MAKING THE PARTS

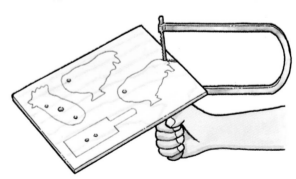

1 Make templates for the parts and transfer onto the plywood. You will need two body pieces. Drill all the holes with the size of bit specified and cut out the pieces with a fretsaw. Sand the pieces smooth.

2 Sand the piece of dowel (4) and test its fit in the large hole in the neck (1) and in the body pieces (2). The fit should be tight in the body holes, but loose enough to allow free movement in the neck. If necessary, enlarge the holes with a round file. Apply a coat of lacquer sealer to all parts and sand lightly.

PAINTING

3 Copying from the photographs, lightly draw the details of the decoration in pencil on both sides of the head and neck, on the outer side of each of the body pieces, and on the top surface of the base.

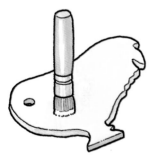

4 Use a stiff brush to stipple white paint on the outsides of the body pieces. Don't completely cover the surface. Allow to dry.

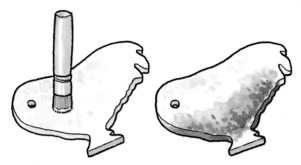

5 Mix some pale blue paint and apply it with an almost dry brush over the white paint. When this is dry, apply some darker blue paint in the same way, but even more sparingly. The overall effect should be lightly speckled.

6 Paint the tail black. When it is dry, apply blue and white paint in long brushstrokes to represent tail feathers. Use orange for the legs and feet and plain blue for the insides of the body pieces and the spacer.

7 Paint both sides of the neck in a similar fashion to the body. Use red for the comb and wattle, and yellow for the beak. The eye is a small black triangle. Paint the base in colors of your choice.

ASSEMBLY

8 Glue the neck dowel into the hole in one of the body pieces so that one end is flush with the outer surface.

9 Glue the spacer onto the inside of the body piece so that the short side aligns with the base of the feet.

10 Slide the neck piece onto the dowel. Glue the second body piece onto the dowel and spacer, making sure it aligns properly with the first body piece. Allow to dry.

11 Glue the hen to the base in the position shown, with the tail at the handle end of the base. Allow to dry. Drill a ¼-inch hole through the base and into the spacer and insert a screw to strengthen the assembly.

12 Clamp the bead in a vise and use a tenon saw to make two grooves on opposite sides of the bead. Cut the string into two equal lengths. Tie one to each of the small holes in the neck. Thread the ends through the holes in the base. Tie the free ends through the wooden bead as shown.

13 Touch up paintwork on dowel ends and elsewhere as necessary. Apply two coats of varnish to all external painted surfaces.

· BOAT ON THE OCEAN ·

This toy is just the thing for sailors of all ages who don't want to get their feet wet! As you turn the handle, the brightly painted ocean liner bobs its way through the rolling waves. The movement of the water is produced by the action of cams on a shaft. Vivid primary colors and strong shapes contribute to the bold impact of this toy.

MATERIALS

⅛in birch plywood
¾ × 1½in

Softwood
5 × ¾ × 25in

⅜in dowel
20in

³⁄₁₆in dowel
1¼in

⅛in dowel
4¾in

White wood glue

Masking tape

Toy-safe paints

Varnish

EQUIPMENT

Fretsaw

Tenon saw

Sandpaper

Drill and bits
⅛in, ³⁄₁₆in, ⅜in spade bit

Round file (optional)

Compass

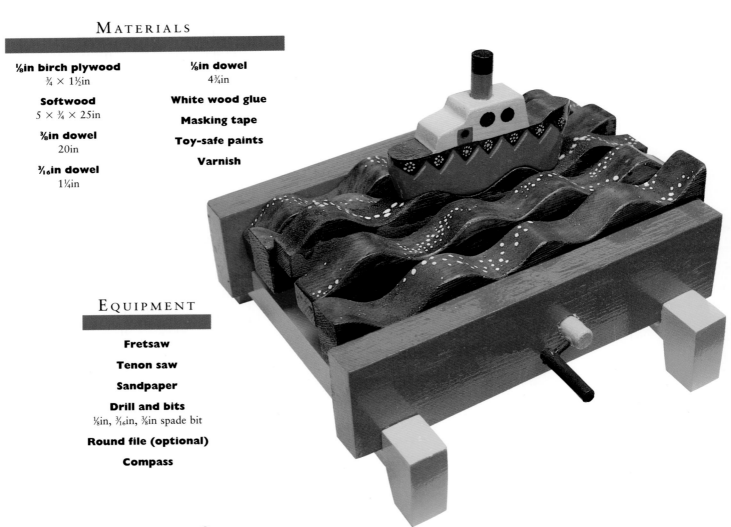

TEMPLATES AND PLANS

These templates are shown half size, or 1:2. Use the elevation as a guide
to shaping the boat.

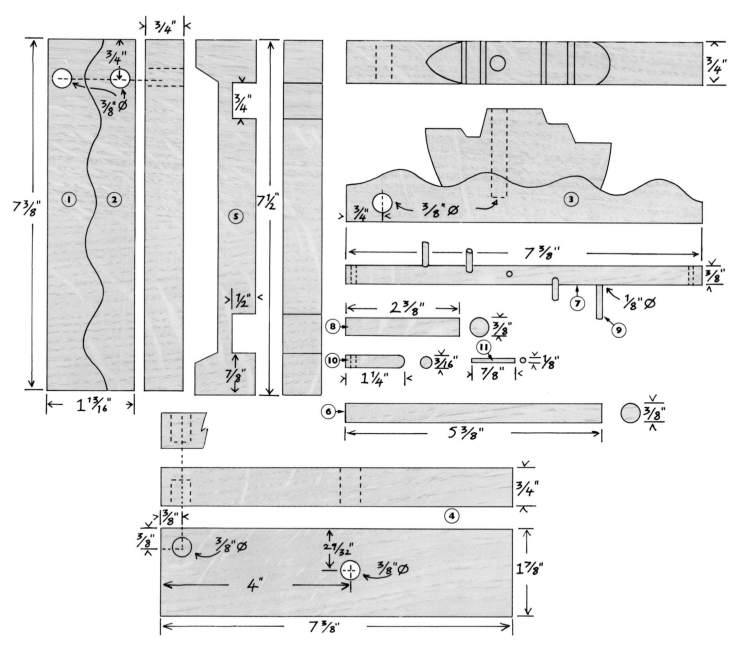

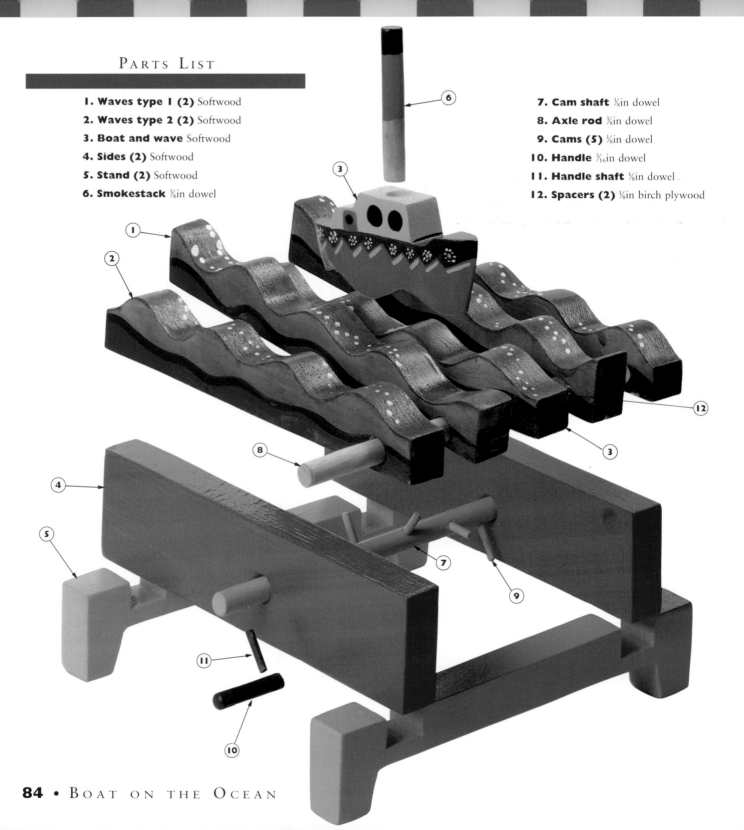

1. **Waves type 1 (2)** Softwood
2. **Waves type 2 (2)** Softwood
3. **Boat and wave** Softwood
4. **Sides (2)** Softwood
5. **Stand (2)** Softwood
6. **Smokestack** ⅜in dowel

7. **Cam shaft** ⅜in dowel
8. **Axle rod** ⅜in dowel
9. **Cams (5)** ⅛in dowel
10. **Handle** ³⁄₁₆in dowel
11. **Handle shaft** ⅛in dowel
12. **Spacers (2)** ⅛in birch plywood

MAKING THE PARTS

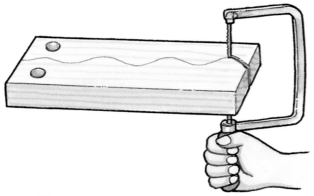

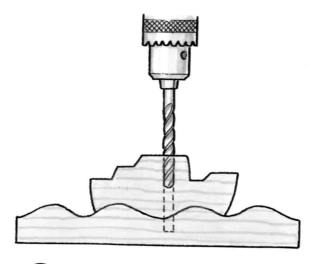

1 Cut the softwood with a tenon saw as shown. Mark a wavy line through the center of each part A. Mark and drill two ⅜-inch holes at one end of each of these parts, as shown. Cut along the undulating line to make four wave sections (1 and 2). Sand smooth.

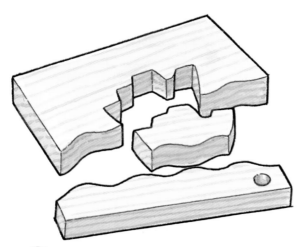

2 Mark out the central wave and boat (3) on the softwood. Cut along the line of the wave and drill a ⅜-inch hole in one end to align with the holes in the other wave pieces. Cut out the boat.

3 Tape the boat back into its original position on its wave and drill through the boat and partway through the wave with a ⅜-inch bit. Separate the parts.

4 Clamping the boat in a vise, plane it to the shape shown, and sand smooth.

5 Cut a 7-inch length of ⅜-inch dowel for the cam shaft (7). Drill five holes in a spiral around the shaft to a depth of 3/16 inch. The easiest way to judge the positions of the holes is to drill the first hole, measure the distance to the next hole, just under 1 inch, and then turn the dowel until the first hole is only just visible. Mark and drill the second hole at this point. Mark and drill the other holes in the same way.

6 Cut six ⅝-inch lengths of ⅛-inch dowel. Glue five of these into the holes in the middle of the shaft, leaving the end holes free. These cams should protrude by about ⅜ inch.

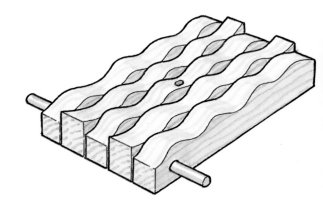

7 Drill a ⅜-inch hole with a spade bit through the center of each side piece (4) and to a depth of about ⅝ inch in one (inside) corner of each piece, as shown. Insert the ends of the cog shaft (7) through the central holes of the two side pieces so that the recessed holes are opposite each other, facing in. Check that the shaft moves freely. Enlarge the holes with a round file if necessary.

8 Cut a 4⅞-inch length of ⅜-inch dowel for the axle rod (8). Draw two ¾-inch diameter circles for the spacers (12) on the plywood. Drill a ⅜-inch hole through the center of each, and cut out using a fretsaw. Arrange the wave pieces along the rod, alternating wave types and with the boat wave in the middle and the spacers on either side, as shown. Make sure that the waves move freely around the axle.

9 Cut two stand pieces (5) from the softwood. Use a tenon saw to cut the basic rectangle and a fretsaw to cut the angled undersides. Cut the slots in the top of each piece (see Basic Techniques).

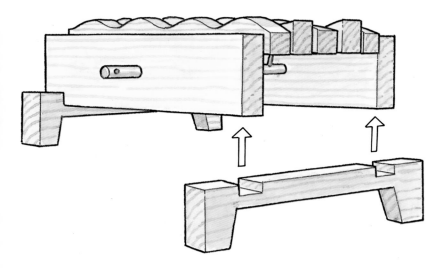

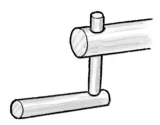

10 Position the axle rod and wave assembly between the side pieces, with the ends of the axle located in the recessed holes in the sides. Place the assembly on the stand with the sides resting in the slots.

13 Make the handle from a 1¼-inch length of ³⁄₁₆-inch dowel, through which you have drilled a ⅛-inch hole. Glue the shaft made from a ¾-inch length of ⅛-inch dowel into the handle.

11 Turn the cam shaft to test the movement of the waves; each wave section should rise up in turn. You may need to adjust the positions of the wave pieces and cam shaft to find the optimum position. When everything is working well, make a pencil mark on the outer ends of the shaft where they emerge from the sides.

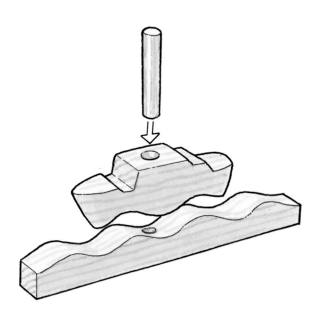

12 Dismantle the assembly. Drill a ⅛-inch hole through the cam shaft close to one of the marks. Insert the remaining ⅝-inch length of ⅛-inch dowel as a retainer. Drill another hole for the handle at the other end of the shaft about ⅛ inch from the mark towards the end.

14 Make the smokestack, which also holds the boat in position, from a 2½-inch length of ⅜-inch dowel. This should fit snugly through the hole in the boat and into the hole in the central wave. Glue into the boat as shown, leaving the lower end protruding.

15 When you are happy with the assembly, dismantle any unglued parts. Apply two coats of white to all parts that will be visible.

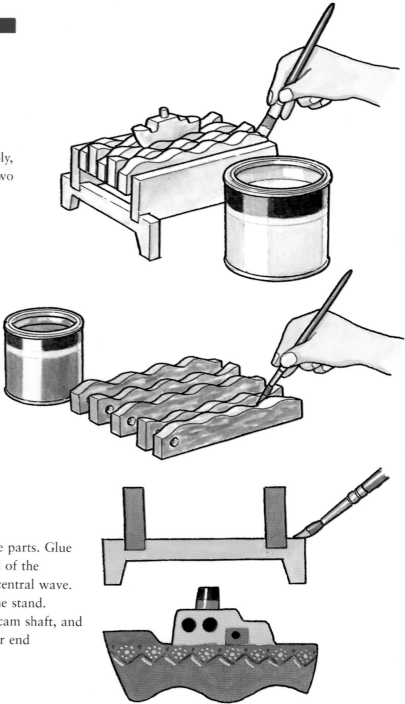

16 Use different shades of blue on the waves to give a realistic sea effect. Add dots of white to the tops of some of the waves to represent surf. Leave to dry, then varnish all external surfaces. As the boat is the focal point of the toy, make it as colorful and detailed as possible.

17 When dry, reassemble the parts. Glue the protruding lower end of the smokestack into the hole in the central wave. Glue the sides into the slots in the stand. Finally, glue the handle into the cam shaft, and the retaining dowel into the other end of the shaft.

· TWIZZLE ·

The movement of this colorful toy is produced by the turning force of twisted rubber bands in conjunction with the centrifugal action of two beads on threads. Simply turn the wire handle at the base of the toy to wind up the mechanism, stand it upright and watch the fish turn, pause and turn again. Uncomplicated to make, this toy will amuse adults and children alike. Like many toys with moving parts, it is best to make and assemble the parts to check the mechanism before painting and carrying out the final assembly.

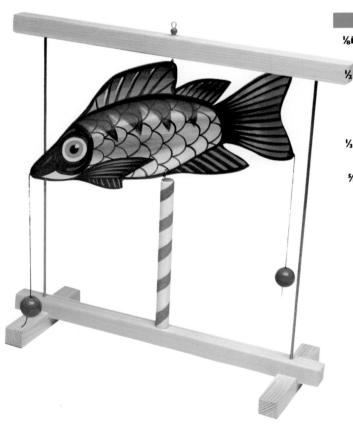

MATERIALS

⅛in birch plywood
10 × 5in

½ × ½in softwood
30in

³⁄₃₂in brass rod
10in

¹⁄₃₂in welding wire
12in

⁵⁄₁₆in birch dowel
8in

Rubber bands
(× 2)
3 × ¹⁄₁₆in

Construction paper
5 × 4in

Scrap hard plastic

Wooden beads
³⁄₁₆in, ⅝in

Button thread

Matchsticks

Toy-safe paints

White wood glue

Varnish

EQUIPMENT

Fretsaw

Tenon saw

Drill and bits
³⁄₆₄in, ¹⁄₁₆in, ³⁄₃₂in, spade ⅜in

Mini drill chuck

Round-nosed pliers

Wire cutters

Craft knife

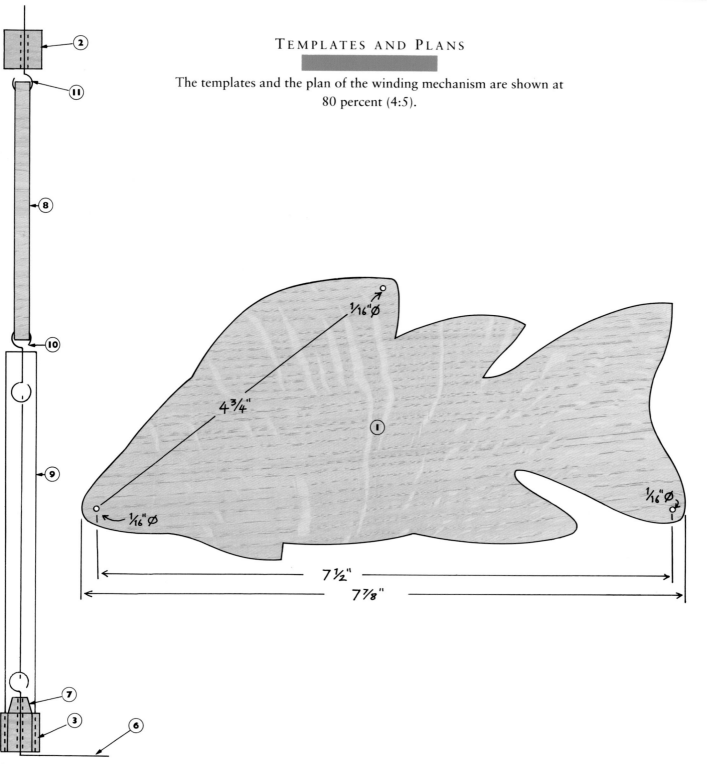

TEMPLATES AND PLANS

The templates and the plan of the winding mechanism are shown at
80 percent (4:5).

② ⑪ ⑧ ⑩ ⑨ ⑦ ③ ⑥

½6" Ø

4¾"

①

½6" Ø

½6" Ø

7½"

7⅞"

PARTS LIST

1. **Fish** ⅛in birch plywood
2. **Frame top** ½in softwood
3. **Frame base** ½in softwood
4. **Frame feet** (2) ½in softwood
5. **Post** (2) ³⁄₃₂in brass rod
6. **Winding handle** ¹⁄₃₂ welding wire
7. **Winding handle bearing** ⁵⁄₁₆in birch dowel
8. **Rubber bands** (2)
9. **Rubber-band tube** Construction paper
10. **Band hook** ¹⁄₃₂in welding wire
11. **Swivel shaft** ¹⁄₃₂in welding wire
12. **Fish swivel washers** (2) Hard plastic
13. **Fish swivel shaft bead**
14. **Thread**
15. **Thread retainers** (2) Matchsticks
16. **Weights** (2) Wooden beads

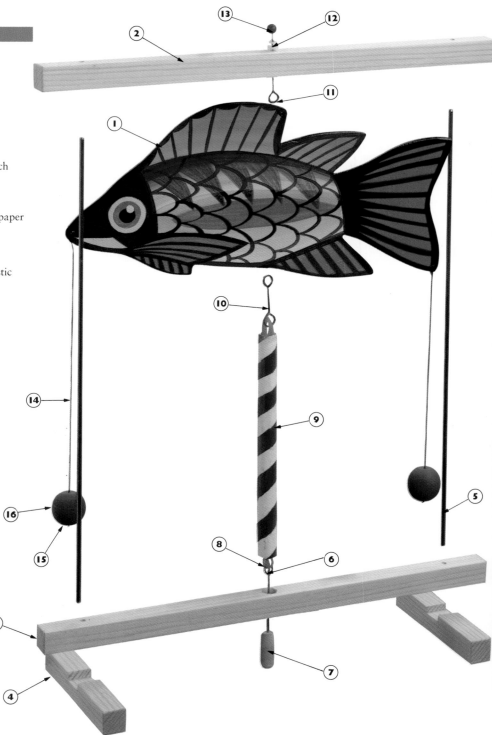

MAKING THE PARTS

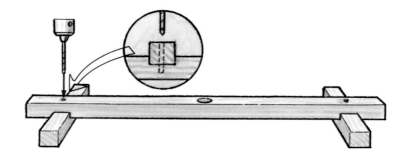

1 Apply two coats of white paint to both sides of the birch plywood, sanding between coats. Allow to dry. Cut out the fish (1) from the plywood with a fretsaw, using the template as a guide. Drill the marked holes using a $\frac{1}{16}$-inch bit. Sand edges.

4 Locate the frame base in the notches of the feet sections so that the center point of each foot is 1 inch from the end of the frame base. Drill through the base and partway through the feet – a total depth of about $\frac{3}{4}$ inch – using a $\frac{3}{32}$-inch bit.

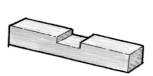

2 Cut two $3\frac{1}{2}$-inch lengths from the softwood for the feet of the frame (4). In each piece, cut a notch the same width as the wood to a depth of $\frac{3}{16}$ inch.

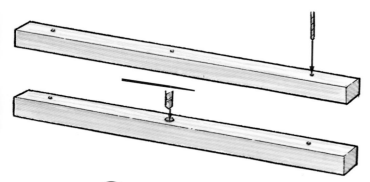

3 Cut two 10-inch lengths of softwood for the frame top and base (2 and 3). Drill a hole through the center of the frame top using a $\frac{3}{32}$ inch bit. Measure $4\frac{1}{8}$ inches from the center on both sides of the center and drill to a depth of $\frac{3}{8}$ inch. Drill a $\frac{3}{8}$ inch hole through the center of the frame base.

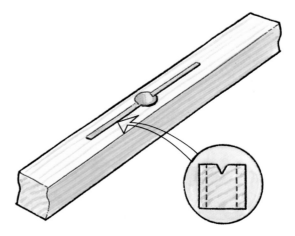

5 Chisel a v-shaped groove $1\frac{3}{16}$ inches long on each side of the center hole in the underside of the frame base, to a depth of about $\frac{1}{8}$ inch.

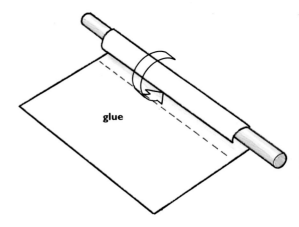

6 Cut the wire into the following lengths: 2¼ inches (swivel shaft – 11); 2 inches (rubber-band hook – 10); 3 inches (winding handle – 6). Use round-nosed pliers to make loops in both ends of the rubber-band hook and in one end of the swivel shaft and the winding handle.

glue

7 To make the winding handle bearing (7), chamfer one end of the ⁵⁄₁₆-inch birch dowel with a craft knife. Measure ¾ inch from the chamfered end and cut. Drill a ³⁄₆₄-inch hole through the center of this piece, and sand to finish.

9 Take a piece of ⁵⁄₁₆-inch dowel and firmly roll the long edge of the construction paper around it once. Spread white glue thinned with water over the rest of the paper and continue to roll it firmly around the dowel. Allow to dry, remove dowel, and trim the tube to a final length of 4¾ inches.

8 Make two plastic washers, about ⅛ inch in diameter, from scrap hard plastic. Drill a hole in the center of each using a ³⁄₆₄-inch bit.

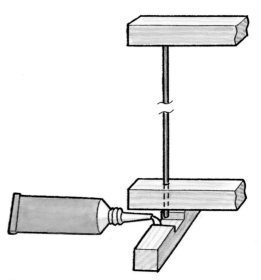

10 Spread a thin layer of wood glue inside the notch on the feet of the frame. Insert the posts (5) through the frame base into the feet and press into position. Locate the frame top on the posts.

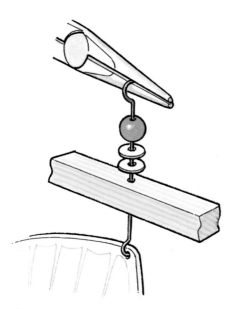

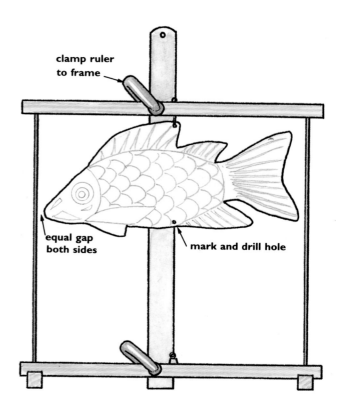

clamp ruler
to frame

equal gap
both sides

mark and drill hole

11 Use pliers to open one of the loops on the wire swivel shaft, and insert it through the middle hole in the dorsal fin of the fish. Close the loop. Insert the shaft up through the hole in the frame top. Thread the washers over the wire and then the ³⁄₁₆-inch wooden bead. Loop the end of the wire to secure the assembly and make sure the fish rotates smoothly.

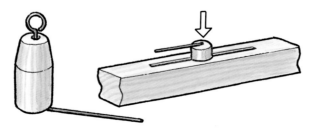

12 Thread the winding handle through the hole in the winding handle bearing so that the existing loop is at the chamfered end. Bend the handle into a right angle as shown and insert through the hole in the frame base so that the handle fits in the groove below.

13 Stand the frame upright, with the fish hanging freely from the top. Mark the position of the lower hole in the fish at a point where it aligns vertically with the top hole and the hole in the center of the frame base. Use a ruler to line up these points. Remember to allow approximately ⅛ inch between the hole and the edge of the fish. The distance between the front of the fish and the post and the tail and the other post should be equal. Drill the hole with a ¹⁄₁₆-inch bit.

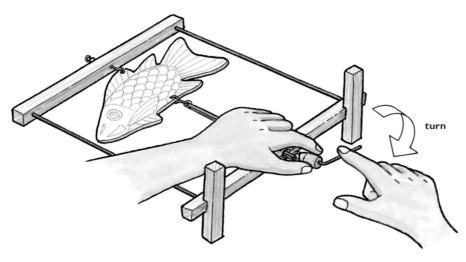

turn

14 Open one loop of the rubber-band hook and insert it through the lower hole in the fish. Close around the hole. Hook two rubber bands onto the other hook and also onto the hook on the winding handle. Lay the assembly down as shown, pull out the handle, and wind for about 20 turns. Stand the assembly upright and make sure the fish rotates freely between the posts.

15 Tie an 8-inch length of heavy (button) thread into each of the holes in the head and tail of the fish, at the notch on the edge of the head and tail. Thread on the ⅝-inch beads and wedge temporarily with a sharpened matchstick about 4 inches along the thread. Trim any excess thread, leaving a little spare under the beads to allow for adjustment.

16 Wind handle; this time try 60 turns to allow approximately 10 minutes of movement. If the fish hits the posts, it may not be balanced properly. If the fish does not swivel easily, check the mobility of the top bearing.

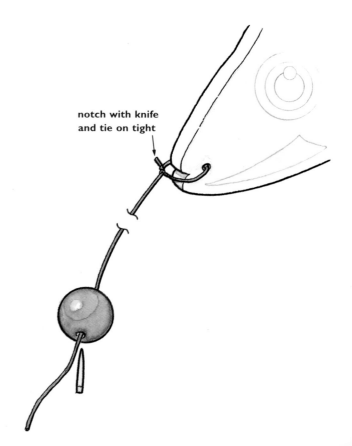

notch with knife
and tie on tight

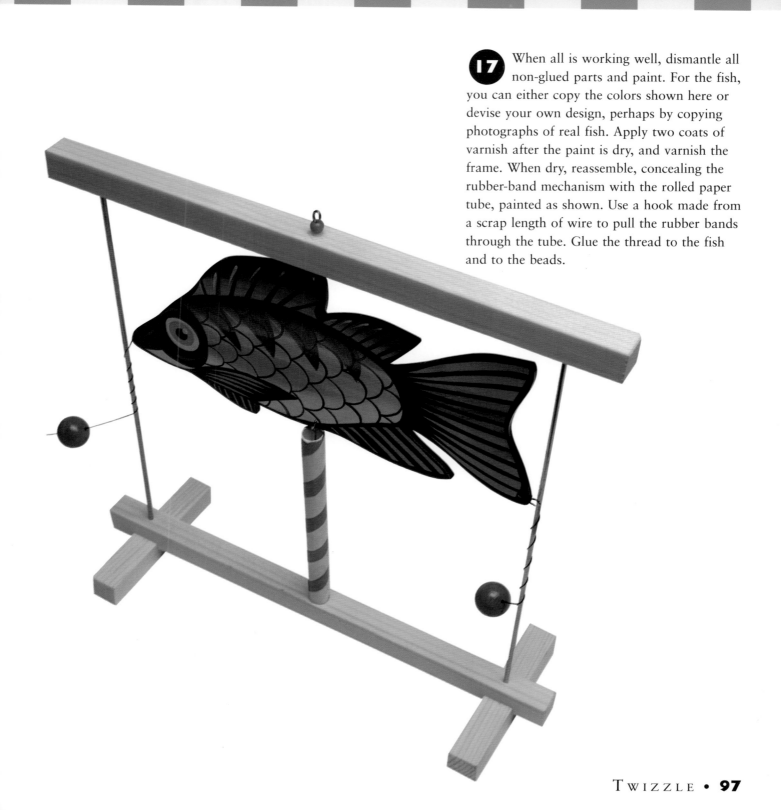

17 When all is working well, dismantle all non-glued parts and paint. For the fish, you can either copy the colors shown here or devise your own design, perhaps by copying photographs of real fish. Apply two coats of varnish after the paint is dry, and varnish the frame. When dry, reassemble, concealing the rubber-band mechanism with the rolled paper tube, painted as shown. Use a hook made from a scrap length of wire to pull the rubber bands through the tube. Glue the thread to the fish and to the beads.

· JUNGLE RACE ·

Based on the intriguing notion that exotic animals like to meet in jungle clearings to hold races, this effective toy is a reworking of the racing games of the 1930s. Just hook the base over the edge of a large table with the animals lined up at the other end. Wind the handle and see which creature reaches the banana-tree winning post first. The element of chance is created by the random way in which the string winds around the shaft. Never mind that this motley band of animals forms a most unlikely gathering, this fantasy game will appeal to the whole family.

MATERIALS

⅜in birch plywood
9 × 9in

⅛in birch plywood
17 × 12in

⁵⁄₁₆in birch dowel
11in

¼ × ¼in maple
6in

Thin braided nylon
cord (size 2A)
9yds

1in wood screws
(× 2)

½in wood screws
(× 4)

½in brads

Toothpicks
(× 10)

White glue

Toy-safe paints

Varnish

EQUIPMENT

Fretsaw

Tenon saw

Drill and bits
³⁄₆₄in, ⁵⁄₆₄in, ³⁄₃₂in, ⁵⁄₃₂in, ⁵⁄₁₆in,
⅜in spade bit

Mini drill chuck

Screwdriver

Round file

Sandpaper

Craft knife

Square

Tape measure or long
ruler

Compass

TEMPLATES AND PLANS

The parts on this page are at 66:7 percent, or 2:3. Those on the next
page are full size.

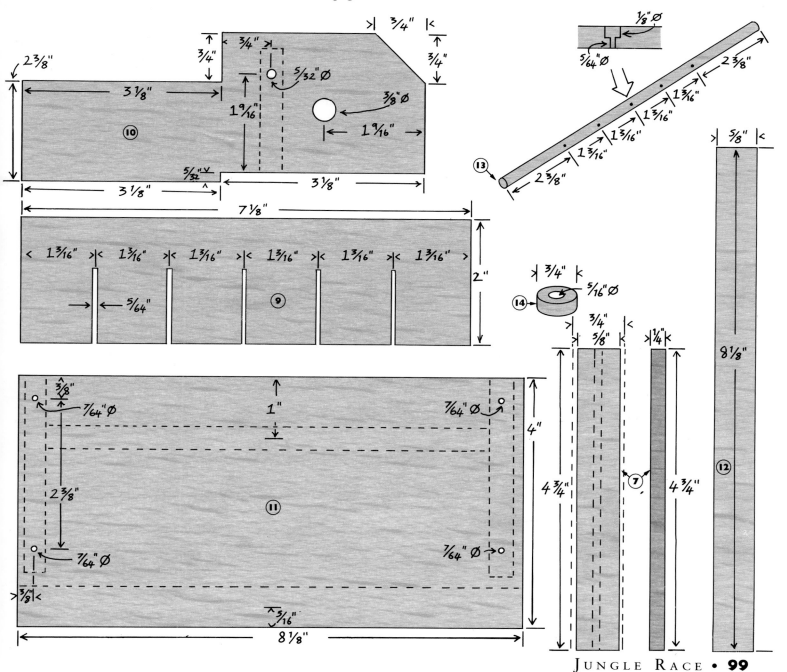

Parts List

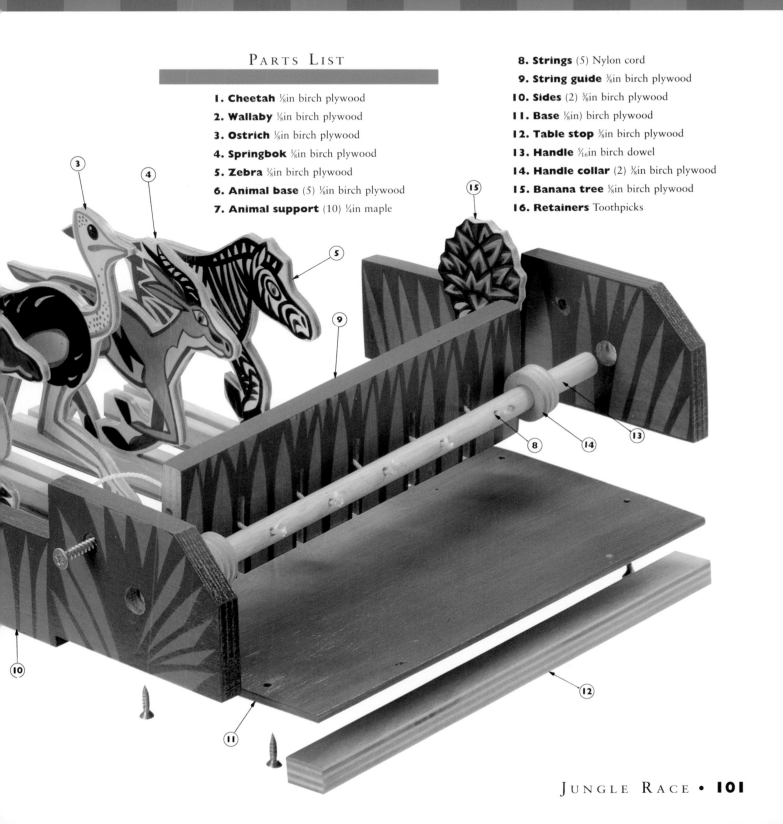

1. **Cheetah** ⅛in birch plywood
2. **Wallaby** ⅛in birch plywood
3. **Ostrich** ⅛in birch plywood
4. **Springbok** ⅛in birch plywood
5. **Zebra** ⅛in birch plywood
6. **Animal base** (5) ⅛in birch plywood
7. **Animal support** (10) ¼in maple
8. **Strings** (5) Nylon cord
9. **String guide** ⅜in birch plywood
10. **Sides** (2) ⅜in birch plywood
11. **Base** ⅛in) birch plywood
12. **Table stop** ⅜in birch plywood
13. **Handle** ⁵⁄₁₆in birch dowel
14. **Handle collar** (2) ⅜in birch plywood
15. **Banana tree** ⅛in birch plywood
16. **Retainers** Toothpicks

MAKING THE PARTS

1 Make templates for all the parts from the diagrams provided, scaling up the sizes where necessary. Cut out the parts and drill any marked holes. Countersink the marked holes in the sides (10), making sure that you drill from the outer side of each piece. Sand all edges.

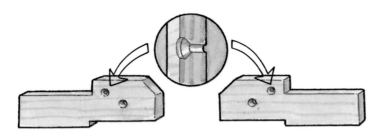

2 Cut the slots in the string guide (9) using a craft knife and tenon saw (see Basic Techniques). Sand the inside edges of the slots smooth so that the cord for the strings slides easily but not too loosely inside.

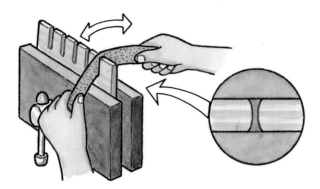

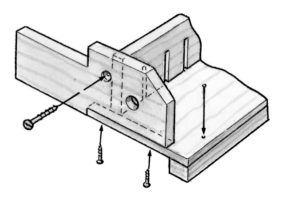

3 Screw the sides to the string guide with two 1-inch wood screws. Attach the table stop (12) to the base (11) with two ½-inch brads nailed through the top of the base, and sand smooth. Join the sides and string guide assembly to the base and secure in position from below with four ½-inch wood screws.

4 Make the handle (13) from a 9½-inch length of ⁵⁄₁₆-inch birch dowel. Drill recessed holes for each of the animal strings, as shown on the plans.

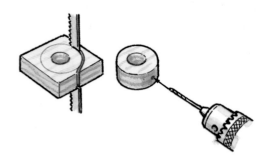

5 Make the two handle collars (14) from ¾-inch diameter circles of ⅜-inch plywood. Drill a hole through the center of each with a ⅜-inch spade bit, cut out with a fretsaw, and sand smooth. Drill a ³⁄₆₄-inch hole in the side of each collar for the retaining pins, as shown.

6 Slide the collars onto the handle and enlarge the holes in the collars if necessary to ensure a sliding fit. Insert the handle and collars through the holes in the sides, making sure the collars are on the inside. Check that the handle spins freely in the holes with a small amount of play. Adjust the position of the shaft and collars so that the handle protrudes from each side by an equal amount. Attach the collars to the handle with the brads.

7 Glue a pair of animal supports (7) to each animal base (6), making sure that the slot between the supports is wide enough for the animal pieces. Place the supports with the straight grain of the ramin along the sides. Sand the base flush to the supports. Drill a hole for the string holder with a $\frac{5}{64}$-inch bit through the sides at the front of both supports.

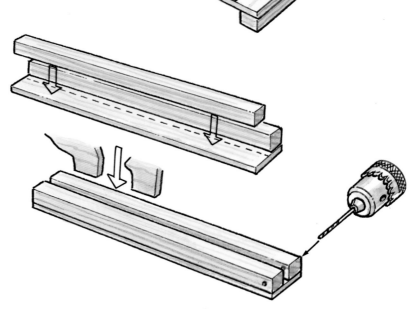

8 Cut the nylon cord into five lengths of 60 inches. Tie one end of each to a retainer made from a piece of toothpick inserted through the front hole in the animal supports, as shown. Trim and seal the ends with a lighted match to prevent fraying.

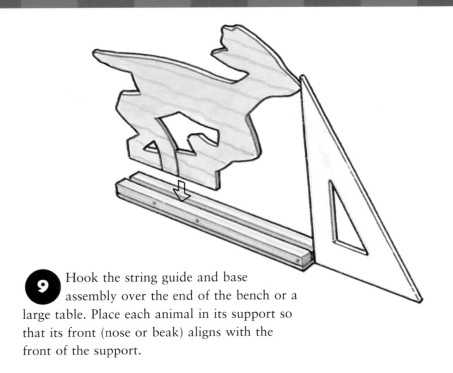

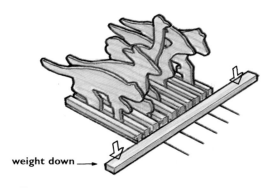

9 Hook the string guide and base assembly over the end of the bench or a large table. Place each animal in its support so that its front (nose or beak) aligns with the front of the support.

weight down →

10 Drill two holes with a ⁵⁄₆₄-inch bit through each animal support with the animal in place, as shown. Line up the animals in their supports on the table top with the fronts of the supports close up against a scrap piece of wood held down with weights to prevent movement. The distance between the edge of the table and the front of the weighted wood should be 50 inches.

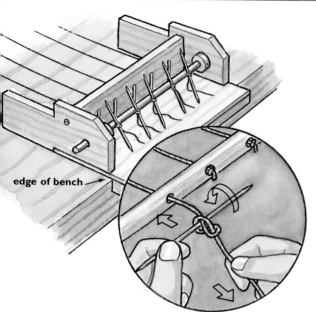

edge of bench →

12 Dismantle all non-glued parts. Remove the strings from the animal supports by pushing out the toothpicks. Apply two coats of white undercoat on both sides of the animals and banana tree, then paint as shown, leaving the edges unpainted. Paint the sides and string holder on both sides in shades of green. Paint the base in brownish greens. When the paint is dry, varnish all parts except the handle assembly. Allow to dry.

13 Cut toothpicks in half and insert in the holes to secure the animals in their supports. Attach the banana tree to one of the sides with two ½-inch brads. Reassemble the other parts as before.

11 Thread the free ends of the strings through the string guide slots and then through the nonrecessed side of the holes in the handle. Secure and adjust the length of each string as follows: pull the string taut; knot the end on the recessed side of the holes and insert toothpicks to secure, as shown; slide the knot down the string until it reaches the hole; trim end and seal with a lighted match; remove toothpicks. After all the strings are tied, check that they are of equal length and tension, and adjust knots as necessary.

· BATHSUB ·

This jolly underwater craft is more than mere decoration – it actually works. Wind up the rubber band-driven propeller, put the submarine in the bathtub and watch it dive under the water just like a real submarine. It uses forward motion, ballast, and a vane to control the depth and angle of the dive. This clever toy will help your child learn about the principles of submarine technology while having fun in the bath (not to mention washing!).

EQUIPMENT

Coping saw

Small hacksaw

Drill and bits
$\frac{5}{64}$in, $\frac{1}{16}$in, $\frac{1}{4}$in

Soldering iron and solder

Metal snips

Scissors

Hammer

Sandpaper

Metal file

Round-nosed pliers

Wire cutters

Compass

Craft knife

MATERIALS

$\frac{1}{2}$in birch plywood
7 × 2$\frac{1}{2}$in

$\frac{1}{4}$in birch dowel
2in

$\frac{1}{8}$in birch plywood
4 × 3in

26 gauge brass sheet
2 × 2in

$\frac{1}{16}$in brass rod
3in

Empty ballpoint pen refill

6in nail

$\frac{1}{16}$ × 3in wide rubber bands
(×3)

$\frac{1}{2}$in brads
(× 4)

Rapid-drying epoxy glue

Varnish

These are full size. Use the templates as positioning guides.

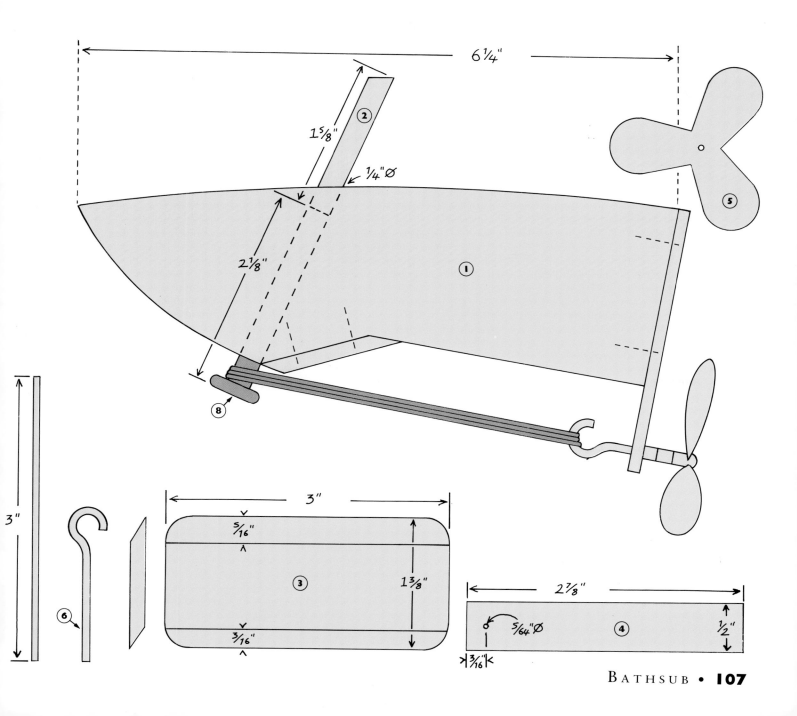

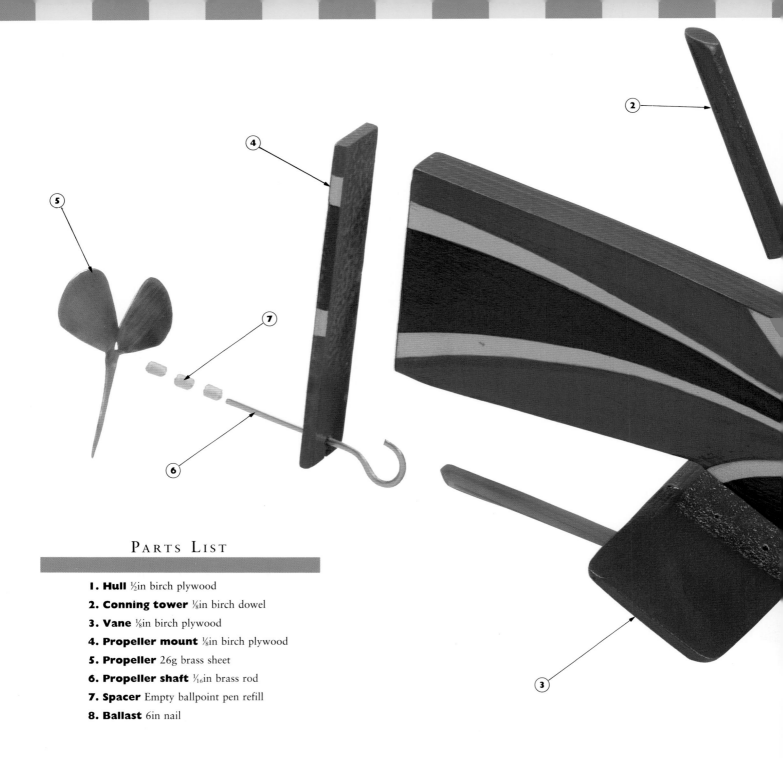

Parts List

1. **Hull** ½in birch plywood
2. **Conning tower** ⅛in birch dowel
3. **Vane** ⅛in birch plywood
4. **Propeller mount** ⅛in birch plywood
5. **Propeller** 26g brass sheet
6. **Propeller shaft** ¹⁄₁₆in brass rod
7. **Spacer** Empty ballpoint pen refill
8. **Ballast** 6in nail

1 Using templates traced from the diagrams, mark and cut out the plywood parts. Smooth the edges.

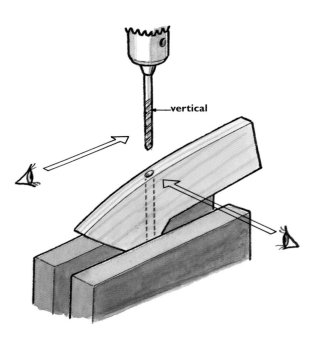

vertical

2 Clamp the hull (1) in a vise, as shown. Using a ¼-inch bit, drill the hole for the conning tower and ballast halfway through the hull, following the line on the template. Make sure that the drill remains parallel to the sides of the hull. Turn the hull around so that the base is uppermost and drill from this side until the two holes meet.

5 Check the fit of the dowel in the hole in the top of the hull. It should be tight but movable. Sand the end if necessary. Apply a generous amount of epoxy glue to the end of the dowel. Place in the hole to a depth of approximately ½ inch and rotate to spread the glue around the hole. Spread the excess glue neatly around the joint and stand the assembly vertically to dry. Then trim the dowel horizontally to a length of 1⅜ inches.

glue

3 Drill the hole marked in the propeller mount (4) with a ⁵⁄₆₄-inch bit. Glue to the back end of the hull and attach with two brads, as shown.

MAKING THE PROPELLER

deburr

chamfer

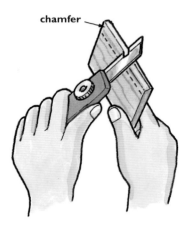

4 Mark chamfer lines on the top, ⁵⁄₁₆ inch, and underside, ³⁄₁₆ inch, of the longer sides of the vane (3), as shown. Cut the chamfers carefully with a craft knife, paring away small amounts at a time. Check that the vane fits snugly under the hull. Trim further as necessary. When the chamfering is complete, smooth with sandpaper.

6 Draw the shape onto a piece of posterboard and cut it out. Attach the board template to the brass sheet with double-sided tape. Scribe the outline and the center hole onto the metal with the compass point and remove the posterboard. Drill the center hole with a ¹⁄₁₆-inch bit, and cut out the propeller with metal snips in stages, as shown. File off any burrs along the edges and polish with steel wool. Paint the shaded area of the prop in any flat color, leaving a circle around the center of about ¼ inch. Leave to dry.

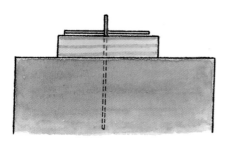

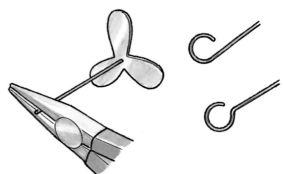

7 Assemble the propeller shaft (6) and the propeller so that the top of the propeller protrudes about ¼ inch. Drill a hole through a scrap of ½-inch plywood. Insert the long end of the propshaft through the hole so that the propeller is supported by the plywood, and clamp the shaft in a vise.

9 Trim the end of the shaft with wire cutters so that it measures 1¾ inches from the underside of the propeller. Using pliers, bend the end of the shaft to form a hook. This is best done in two stages, as shown.

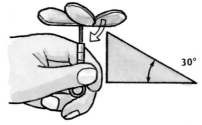

10 Cut three ⅛-inch sections with a craft knife from an empty ballpoint pen refill for the propeller spacers and thread these onto the shaft.

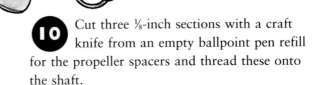

8 Heat the soldering iron and then the propeller joint. Apply the solder, keeping the iron in place, until a neat blob of solder forms around the joint. The paint will keep the solder from flowing onto the propeller blades. If the joint does not form neatly, melt off the solder and try again. When the soldering is complete, wash off the paint and polish the propeller with metal polish.

11 Make a 30° template from a piece of scrap posterboard as a guide to the angle to which to bend the propeller blades. They can be bent quite easily with your fingers to the shape shown.

12 Clamp the nail (8) in a vise and use a hacksaw to cut it to a length of 2⅛ inches from the head. File off any burrs.

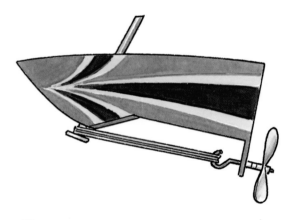

13 Sand all the wooden parts smooth. Hold the hull on a sprue through the hole in the underside while you paint (see Basic Techniques). Paint the hull and vane with two coats in the background color shown. Allow to dry and add the decoration to the hull. When all the paint is dry, apply three coats of varnish for a waterproof finish.

15 Insert the hook on the propeller shaft through the hole on the mount. Insert the ballast in the hole in the underside of the hull. Thread the three rubber bands over the end of the nail and propeller shaft. Wind for 30 turns clockwise and release, making sure that the propeller turns freely.

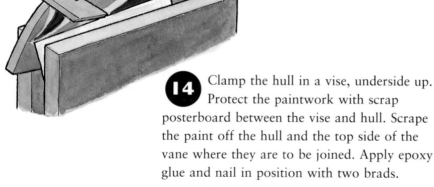

postcard both sides

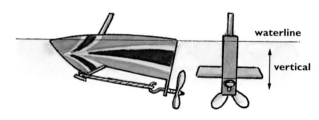

waterline

vertical

14 Clamp the hull in a vise, underside up. Protect the paintwork with scrap posterboard between the vise and hull. Scrape the paint off the hull and the top side of the vane where they are to be joined. Apply epoxy glue and nail in position with two brads.

16 Fill the bathtub with water to at least 12 inches and launch the submarine. Check that it floats as shown and refer to the troubleshooting box if there is a problem.

17 Wind the propeller for 40 turns. Holding the propeller, place the submarine at one end of the bathtub and release. It should submerge and resurface at the other end. Refer to the troubleshooting box if there are problems. When all is working well, glue the ballast in position.

Fault	Cause	Remedy
Submarine too high in water	Too little ballast	Use longer length of nail
Submarine too low in water	Too much ballast	Trim nail ⅛ inch at a time until the submarine floats correctly
Submarine goes forward but does not dive	Too little power	Propeller not turned enough times
	Propeller movement impeded	Check that the hole in the propeller mount is large enough
	Hook not properly aligned	Rebend hook
	Angle of propeller blades too great or too small	Adjust angle of blades

· BIG FAT BIPLANE ·

Recapture the glamour of the early days of flying with this biplane. With decoration and detailing inspired by the aircraft of the 1930s and 40s, this model, with its turning propeller and rolling wheels, will be a big hit with young aircraft enthusiasts. Try personalizing the paintwork by substituting the number with that of the child's age, or by adding his or her name on the fuselage. Some parts of the plane are left unpainted to give the authentic impression of unbleached cotton, so be sure to choose knot-free wood with a pleasing grain.

EQUIPMENT

Fretsaw

Coping saw

Tenon saw

Plane

Drill and bits
¼in, ³⁄₁₆in

Craft knife

Square

Sandpaper and block

½in chisel

Mallet

MATERIALS

⅞in softwood
12 × 12in

⅛in birch plywood
10 × 10in

¼in birch dowel
12in

½in birch dowel
4in

4in nails
(× 2)

Scrap softwood
1½ × 1½ × 3in

Scrap hard plastic or metal washers
(× 4)

Quick-drying epoxy glue

Paints

Varnish

Templates and Plans

All parts, including those in the side elevation, are reproduced at
50 percent, or 1:2.

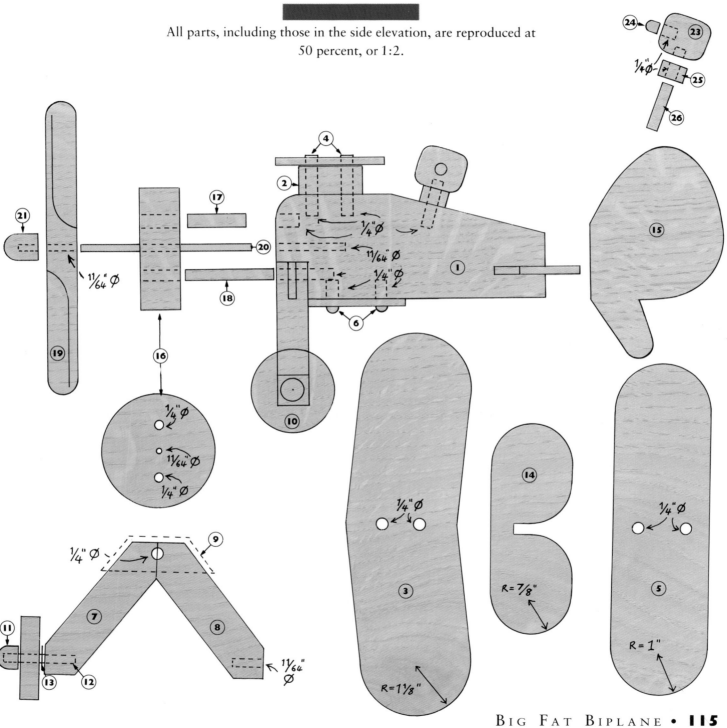

Parts List

1. **Fuselage** ⅞in softwood
2. **Spacer** ⅞in softwood
3. **Top wing** ⅛in birch plywood
4. **Top wing retaining dowels** (2) ¼in birch dowel
5. **Bottom wing** ⅛in birch plywood
6. **Bottom wing retaining dowels** (2) ¼in birch dowel
7. **Undercarriage (right)** ⅝in softwood
8. **Undercarriage (left)** ⅝in softwood
9. **Undercarriage support** ⅛in birch plywood
10. **Wheels** (2) ⅞in softwood
11. **Wheel retainers** (2) ½in birch dowel
12. **Axles** (2) Nail
13. **Wheel axle washers** (2) Hard plastic or metal
14. **Tail** ⅛in birch plywood
15. **Rudder** ⅛in birch plywood
16. **Engine** ⅞in softwood
17. **Engine-retaining dowel** ¼in birch dowel
18. **Engine and undercarriage retaining dowel** ¼in birch dowel
19. **Propeller** ⅞in softwood
20. **Propeller shaft** Nail
21. **Propeller shaft retainer** ½in birch dowel
22. **Propeller shaft washers** (2) Hard plastic or metal
23. **Pilot head** Scrap softwood
24. **Nose** ¼in birch dowel
25. **Neck** ½in birch dowel
26. **Pilot-retaining dowel** ¼in birch dowel

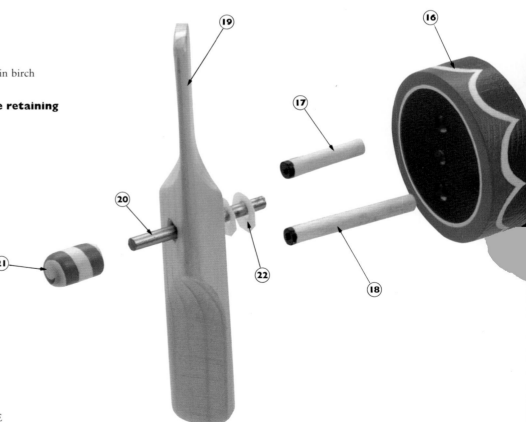

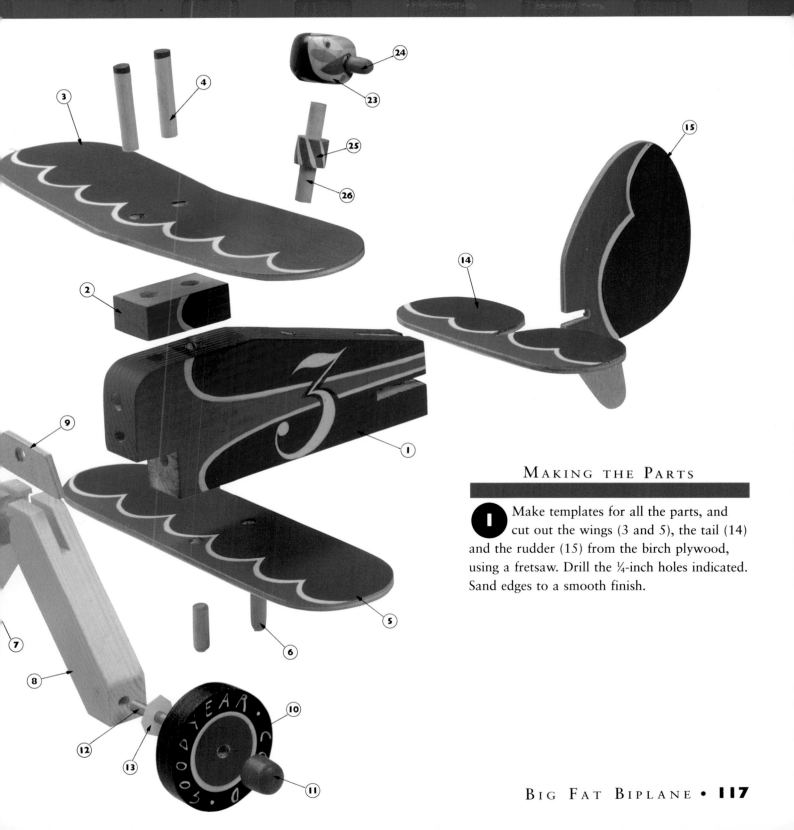

MAKING THE PARTS

1 Make templates for all the parts, and cut out the wings (3 and 5), the tail (14) and the rudder (15) from the birch plywood, using a fretsaw. Drill the ¼-inch holes indicated. Sand edges to a smooth finish.

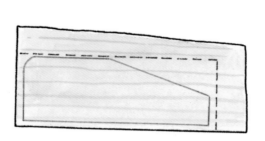

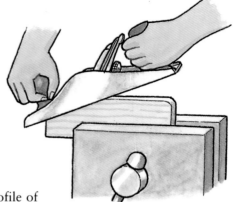

2 Using a craft knife, mark the profile of the fuselage (1) on the softwood so that the grain runs horizontally. Allow an extra ¼ inch at the front and back and an extra ¹⁄₁₆ inch at the top and bottom. Cut out the basic shape with a tenon saw and plane along the grain to the exact size.

THE UNDERCARRIAGE

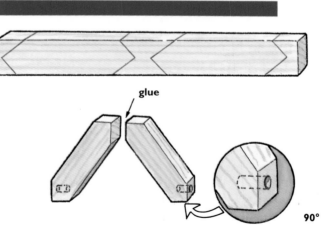

glue

90°

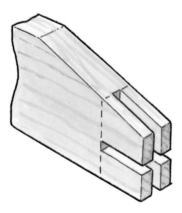

3 Use medium sandpaper to smooth the end grain and to round off the front. Finish with fine sandpaper. Make slots in the tail end as shown.

4 Cut the two parts of the undercarriage (7 and 8) from ⅞-inch softwood planed to ⅝ inch. Drill ¹¹⁄₆₄-inch holes in one facet of one end of each piece to a depth of ⅝ inch, as shown. Make sure the holes are at right angles to the surface.

5 Glue the two pieces together on a flat surface to make the undercarriage.

6 Clamp the undercarriage in a vise and cut a ⅛-inch slot across the top, by making two parallel cuts ¾ inch deep and then removing the waste with a coping saw.

7 Cut out the undercarriage support (9) from the ⅛-inch plywood and glue this into the slot in the undercarriage. When dry, use a craft knife to trim the excess flush to the surface of the undercarriage. Sand smooth.

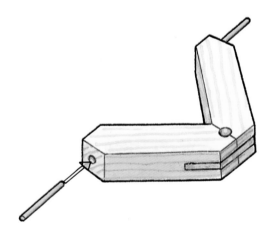

8 Drill a ¼-inch hole through the center of the assembly, as shown. Cut two 1½-inch lengths from a 4-inch nail, removing the head and point. Glue into the holes in the ends of the undercarriage.

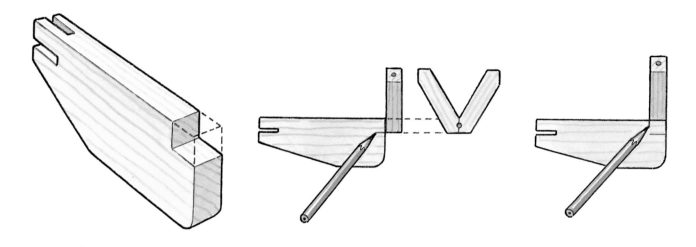

9 Measure and cut the recess for the undercarriage in the fuselage, as shown.

10 With the undercarriage in position in its recess, supported in a vise by scrap softwood, drill through the hole in its center into the fuselage to a depth of ½ inch. Cut two 2-inch lengths of ¼-inch birch dowel and insert one – the engine and undercarriage retainer (18) – into the hole. This should be a snug, but removable fit.

11 To make the engine (16), draw a circle with a radius of 1¼ inches on the ⅞-inch softwood. Cut out with a coping saw and drill the holes indicated. Smooth with fine sandpaper.

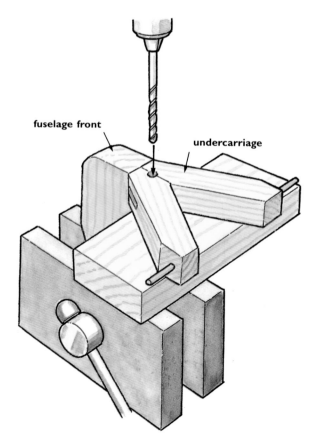

fuselage front

undercarriage

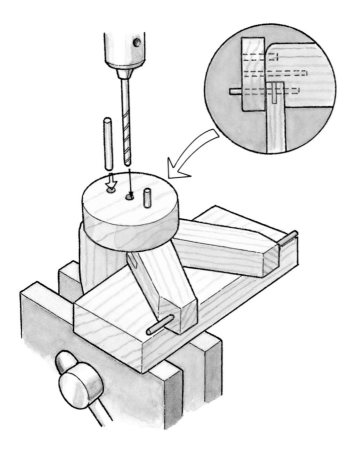

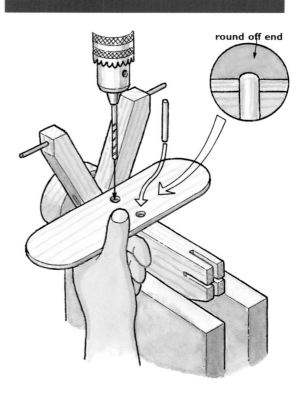

round off end

12 Position one of the larger holes in the engine over the dowel, and drill a hole through the second hole in the engine into the fuselage with a ¼-inch bit to a depth of ½ inch. Insert the second 2-inch-long dowel. Using a ¹¹⁄₆₄-inch bit, drill through the central hole into the fuselage. Insert but do not glue the propshaft (20) into this hole. Remove the engine and undercarriage from the fuselage and glue the two retaining dowels in place. Sand the ends flush to the engine.

13 Position the bottom wing (5) centered on the underside of the fuselage so that it is flush against the undercarriage. Drill through the existing holes in the wing into the fuselage to a depth of ½ inch. Apply glue inside the drilled holes and insert two ¾-inch dowels. Sand the protruding ends of the dowels to a rounded shape.

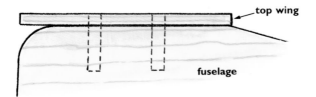

top wing

fuselage

14 Position the top wing (3) on the top of the fuselage, and drill through the existing holes into the fuselage with a ¼-inch bit to a depth of ½ inch.

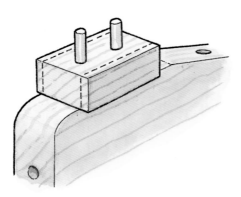

15 Make the wing spacer from a piece of softwood 1¾ × ⅝ × 1⅛ inches. Position this under the top wing and drill all the way through, using the holes in the wing as a guide.

17 Drill a hole for the pilot in the top of the fuselage using a ¼-inch bit to a depth of ½ inch.

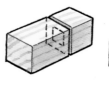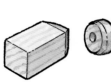

18 Shape the pilot's head from a scrap of softwood approximately 1½ × 1½ × 6 inches. Make saw cuts to a depth of ½ inch around the piece along a line 1¼ inches from one end, as shown. Make diagonal cuts on each side of the first cut and across the end of the piece. Use a craft knife to shape the head further and smooth with medium sandpaper. Cut the head from the scrap wood and drill a hole for the neck and nose with a ¼-inch bit. Cut a 1-inch scrap of ¼-inch dowel for the retainer.

16 Mount the spacer in position on the fuselage with two 1⅜-inch lengths of ¼-inch dowel. Plane and sand the spacer flush to the sides of the fuselage, then remove the spacer, trim the ends, and sand to finish. Glue the dowels into the spacer so that a short length protrudes to locate in the wing holes, and glue the spacer assembly to the top wing. Sand dowel ends flush to the wings.

19 Cut one ¾-inch and two ⅜-inch lengths of ½-inch dowel for the propshaft retainer (21) and wheel retainers (11). Shape each piece as follows. Always wear thick gloves for this: insert a length of 4-inch nail, from which you have removed the head, firmly into the exact center of the dowel. Secure the free end of the nail in the drill chuck. Resting the drill on the bench and holding the end of the dowel against a pad of medium sandpaper, start the drill on slow. Using a turning action, sand the dowel end to a round shape.

Making the Propeller

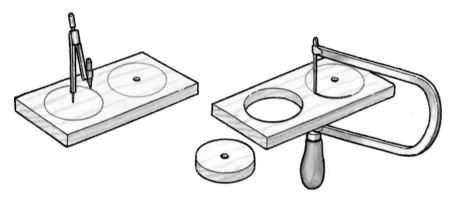

20 Plane a 2 × 4-inch piece of ⅞-inch softwood to a thickness of ⅜ inch. Draw two circles for the wheels (10) with a radius of ⅞ inch and drill a hole in the center of each with a ³⁄₁₆-inch bit. Cut out with a fretsaw, as shown. Sand the rims, using the method described in step 19, but with a sanded-down piece of ¼-inch dowel in place of the nail.

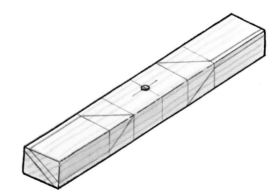

21 Mark the propeller blank on a piece of softwood ⅞ × 6 × ⅝ inches, as shown. Drill the center hole with a ³⁄₁₆-inch bit.

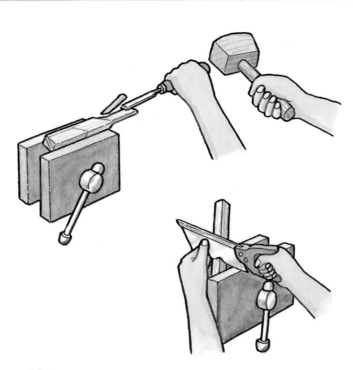

24 Insert a length of ⅛-inch wire rod through the hole in the propeller and support it as shown to check the balance. Sand further if necessary.

ASSEMBLY

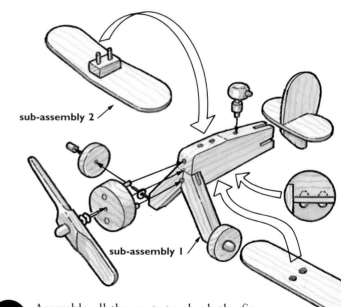

sub-assembly 2

sub-assembly 1

22 Holding the blank in a vise at a slight angle, make the four angled cuts (marked A) with a tenon saw. With the propeller now secured horizontally at a slight angle, remove the rest of the unwanted wood (shaded in the illustration) with a chisel.

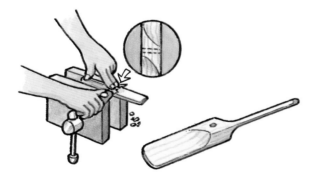

23 Shape the angled cuts into curves with a craft knife. Round off the ends with medium sandpaper and use fine sandpaper to smooth all edges.

25 Assemble all the parts to check the fit and that the propeller and wheels move easily on their shafts. Dismantle, paint, and apply two coats of varnish.

26 Scrape any paint and varnish off surfaces to be glued to ensure good adhesion. Reassemble and glue with rapid-drying epoxy glue in the following order: undercarriage and engine to the fuselage; bottom wing, tail, and rudder to fuselage; top wing and spacer to fuselage; propeller and wheels (unglued) onto their shafts with plastic or metal washers in place; propeller- and wheel-retainers to their shafts (insert cardboard spacers to prevent glue from getting on the propeller and wheels).

· SLITHERING SNAKE ·

Jointed snakes of this kind have a long pedigree. Often made in Asia from bamboo or pithwood, this version uses the more easily obtainable softwood and plywood. The subtle upward curve of the body produces a remarkably realistic snake-like movement.

EQUIPMENT

Small hacksaw

Fretsaw

Block plane

Square

Needle-nosed pliers

Wire cutters

Drill and bits
$\frac{1}{16}$in, $\frac{3}{64}$in, $\frac{1}{4}$in

Mini drill chuck

C-clamp

Sandpaper

Compass

MATERIALS

2 × 1in Knot-free softwood
50in

⅛in birch plywood
6 × 6in

¼in dowel
60in

¾₄in welding wire
39in

Red plastic electric cable
50mm (2in)

1½in brads
(× 2)

Toy-safe paints

Varnish

White wood glue

Posterboard

TEMPLATES AND PLANS

The scale here for all parts is 80 percent, or 4:5.

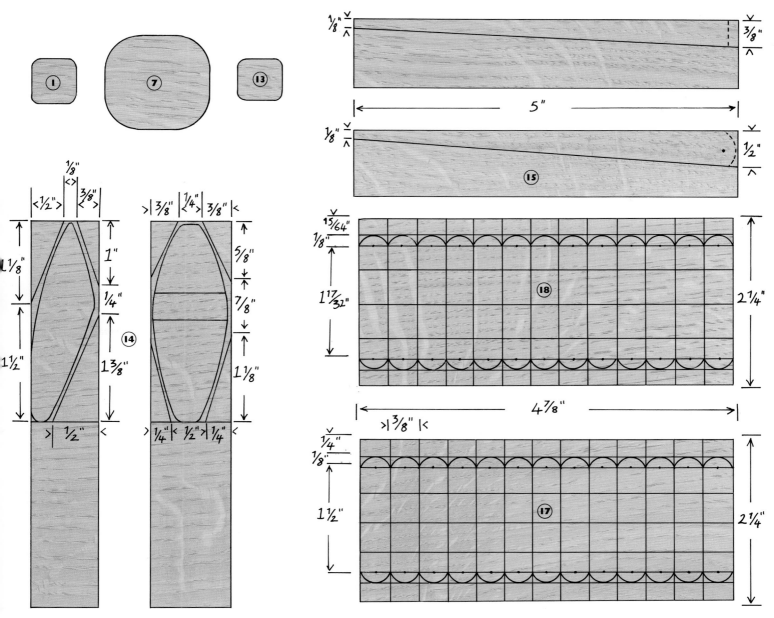

Parts List

1–13. Body segments Softwood

14. Head Softwood

15. Tail Softwood

16. Tongue Red electric cable

17. Top joints (13) ⅛in birch plywood

18. Bottom joints (13) ⅛in birch plywood

19. Pivot shafts (14) Welding wire

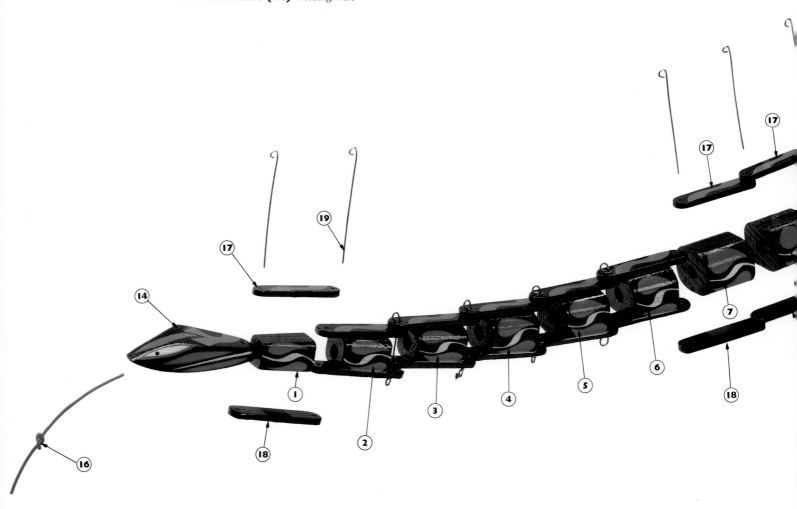

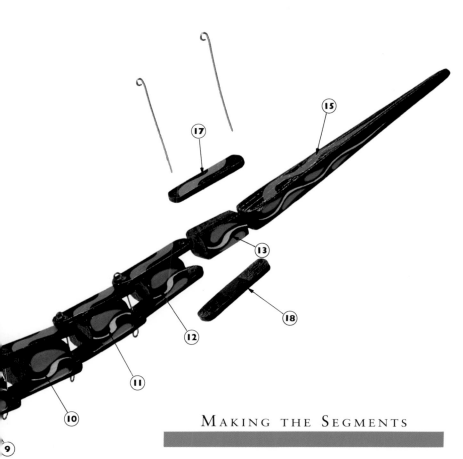

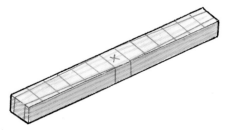

2 Make two marks ½ inch apart in the center of each end of the wood. Draw lines on the top and bottom sides of the wood from these marks to the edges of the middle segment as shown.

3 Clamp the piece in a vise and plane down to the lines. Do not plane the middle segment.

MAKING THE SEGMENTS

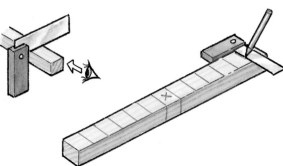

1 Cut a ⅞ × 13-inch piece of the softwood for the body segments (1–13). Along the top edge mark thirteen 1-inch divisions, as shown. Put an "x" in the middle one for reference and mark this segment on all sides of the wood.

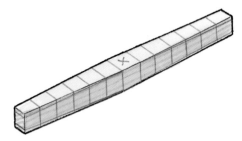

4 Using a square and the lines on the top edge as a guide, mark the rest of the segments on all sides of the piece. Mark the ends, and draw lines on the tapered sides of the wood from these marks to the edges of the middle segment, as shown. Clamp in a vise and plane down to the marked lines as before.

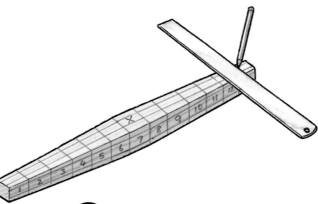

5 Redraw the lines marking the segments that have been planed away. Along the center of each side, draw two further parallel lines ⅜ inch apart. Number the segments along one side for reference.

6 With the piece in a vise as before, plane along the corners to the level marked by the parallel lines. Be careful not to plane away the lines on the top and bottom.

7 Use a small hacksaw with a sharp blade to separate the segments, following the drawn lines as accurately as possible. Lay a sheet of medium sandpaper on the bench, and sand both ends of each segment. Mark the center of the sanded end of each segment. Drill through each one using a ¼-inch bit.

MAKING THE JOINTS

The different hole spacing on the top and bottom sections gives the essential bias.

8 Mark the plywood following the measurements on page 127 exactly. Use a posterboard template to draw the curves. Mark the top joints (17) with a "t" and the bottom ones (18) with a "b." Use the point of a compass to prick the hole positions.

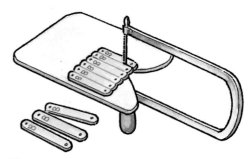

9 Drill the holes using a ³⁄₆₄-inch bit. Using a fretsaw and mount, cut around the curves of each of the joints, and then cut between the curves to separate the joints. Smooth edges with fine sandpaper.

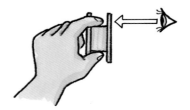 

10 Glue each top joint to a body segment. Position the joints between the parallel lines on each body segment so that the segment is also between the guidelines marked on the joint. When the glue is dry, glue the bottom joints in the same way, so that the joints align as accurately as possible.

MAKING THE HEAD AND TAIL

11 Cut a 5-inch piece of 1 × 2-inch softwood in half lengthwise to make two pieces measuring 1 × 1 × 5 inches. Mark the shape of the head on the top and sides of one of the pieces, following the diagrams and measurements shown on page 127.

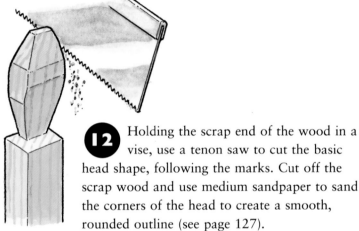

12 Holding the scrap end of the wood in a vise, use a tenon saw to cut the basic head shape, following the marks. Cut off the scrap wood and use medium sandpaper to sand the corners of the head to create a smooth, rounded outline (see page 127).

13 Use a craft knife to chamfer the two eye positions. Drill a ³⁄₆₄-inch hole through the head ⅛ inch from the base. Drill a ¹⁄₁₆-inch hole at an angle in the underside of the head to a depth of ½ inch for the tongue (16).

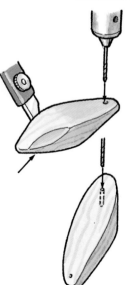

14 Use the scrap softwood for the tail, marking the sides as shown on page 127. Clamp the piece to the workbench and remove the scrap from the side with a tenon saw. Plane smooth. Mark the top of the tail on the top surface and cut the shape as before. Smooth the curved edges with sandpaper. Drill a ³⁄₆₄-inch hole through the top of the tail about ⅛ inch from the front.

PAINTING

15 Cut fifteen 4-inch lengths of ¼-inch dowel to make sprues. Chamfer both ends of 13 of these to a diameter of ⅛ inch; these are the sprues for the body segments. Drill a ¹⁄₁₆-inch hole in one end of the remaining two, and insert in each a brad with the head snipped off. Chamfer the other end as before; these are the sprues for the head and tail. Make a holder by drilling fifteen ¼-inch holes about 1¾ inches apart in a piece of scrap softwood.

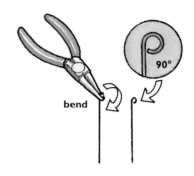

bend   90°

17 Remove any paint clogging the pivot holes by redrilling. Cut the welding wire into fourteen 2¼-inch lengths. Use needle-nosed pliers to bend one end of each piece of wire into a loop ⅛ inch in diameter, as shown.

18 Lay out all the parts in their correct order. Although the numbers will be painted over, you should be able to judge this by their size. Make sure that the shorter top joints are on top.

16 After applying a white undercoat, paint all parts as shown, or design your own snake-like markings. Paint the background color first and allow to dry before adding the markings in stages, as shown. To ensure that the pattern is the same on both sides of each segment, paint one side first and then turn the segment, keeping the sprue on the same side, and paint the other side exactly the same. When dry, apply two coats of varnish.

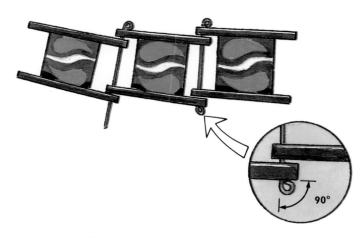

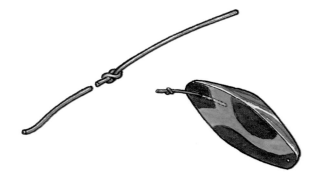

19 Pass a pivot shaft through the holes in the joints between segments 1 and 2. Make a posterboard template $\frac{7}{16}$ inch wide to measure the length of the protruding shaft. Trim with wire cutters to this length. Make a loop in the end as before, allowing a $\frac{1}{16}$-inch clearance between the loop and the side of the joint. Continue to join all the segments in this way, finishing with the head and tail.

20 Tie a half-hitch knot in the red cable, as shown, and trim to length for the tongue. Use white wood glue to attach it into the hole in the underside of the head.

· PUFFIN ·

This "fertility" toy is a charming variation on the laying hens that were produced in Germany in the last century. The design is very popular with toddlers, who are intrigued by the way in which the eggs placed inside the puffin magically reappear when the body is pressed down. However, with young children, it is advisable to keep this toy for special sessions of supervised play, to avoid the risk of rough handling damaging the bird or its mechanism.

MATERIALS

½in birch plywood
4 × 4in

⅜in birch plywood
12 × 12in

⅛in birch plywood
12 × 12in

¹⁄₁₆in birch plywood
20 × 4in

¼in birch dowel
24in

¹⁄₁₆in brass rod
3in

³⁄₃₂in brass rod
6in

20 and 22g piano wire
6in

22g brass sheet
3 × 3in

Scrap softwood

Tinplate from oil can
4 × 2in

1in birch balls
(× 5)

1½in wood screws
(× 2)

½in wood screws
(× 2)

½in brads

Toy-safe paints

White wood glue or
rapid-drying epoxy
resin

Sewing pins

Auto-body filler

EQUIPMENT

Fretsaw

Tenon saw

Drill and bits
³⁄₆₄in, ¹⁄₁₆in, ³⁄₃₂in, ⁷⁄₆₄in ³⁄₁₆in,
¼in

Mini drill chuck

Metal snips

Rasp or coarse
sandpaper and dowel

Soldering iron and
solder

Wire cutters

Craft knife

Sandpaper

The body surround (part 3) is 25 percent, or 1:4. The other parts are at 50 percent.

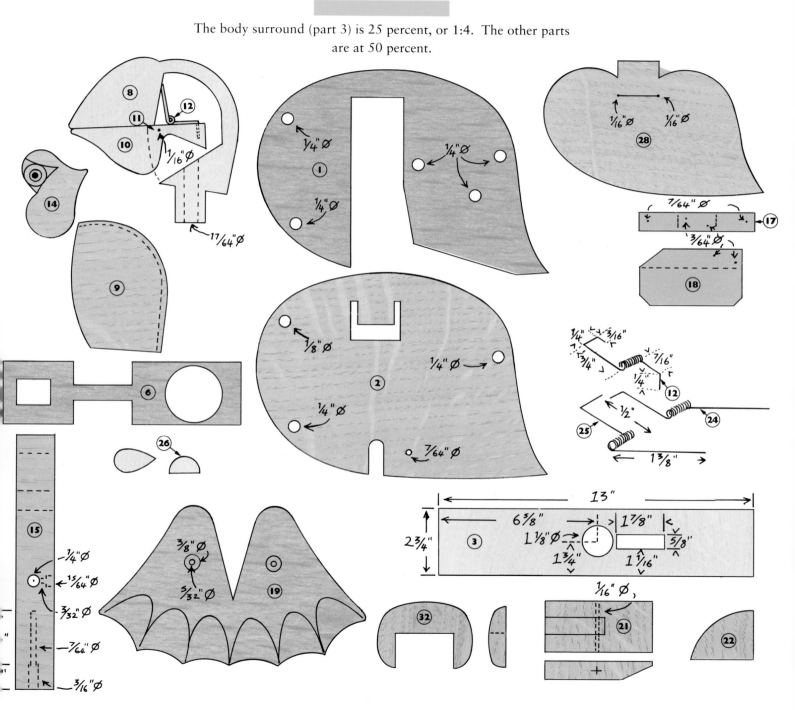

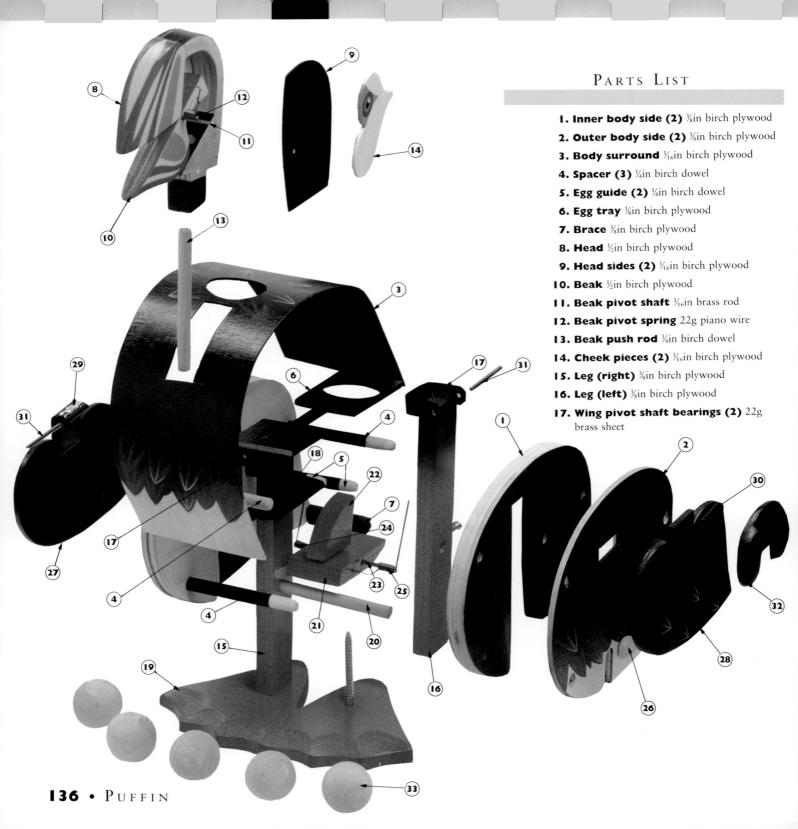

1. **Inner body side (2)** ⅜in birch plywood
2. **Outer body side (2)** ⅛in birch plywood
3. **Body surround** 1⁄16in birch plywood
4. **Spacer (3)** ¼in birch dowel
5. **Egg guide (2)** ¼in birch dowel
6. **Egg tray** ⅛in birch plywood
7. **Brace** ⅜in birch plywood
8. **Head** ½in birch plywood
9. **Head sides (2)** 1⁄16in birch plywood
10. **Beak** ½in birch plywood
11. **Beak pivot shaft** 1⁄16in brass rod
12. **Beak pivot spring** 22g piano wire
13. **Beak push rod** ¼in birch dowel
14. **Cheek pieces (2)** 1⁄16in birch plywood
15. **Leg (right)** ⅜in birch plywood
16. **Leg (left)** ⅜in birch plywood
17. **Wing pivot shaft bearings (2)** 22g brass sheet

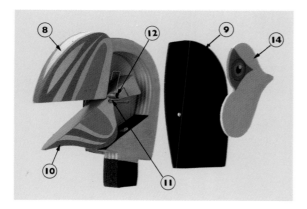

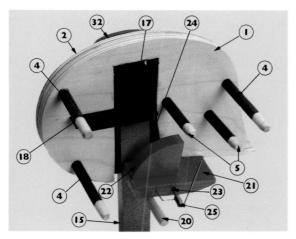

18. **Beak push rod plate** 22g brass sheet

19. **Feet** ⅜in birch plywood

20. **Egg door push rod** ¼in birch dowel

21. **Egg door** ⅜in birch plywood

22. **Egg stop** ⅜in birch plywood

23. **Egg door pivot shaft** ³⁄₃₂in brass rod

24. **Egg door spring (right)** 20g piano wire

25. **Egg door spring (left)** 20g piano wire

26. **Egg door pivot shaft retainers (2)** Softwood

27. **Wing (right)** ⅛in birch plywood

28. **Wing (left)** ⅛in birch plywood

29. **Wing bearing (right)** Tinplate

30. **Wing bearing (left)** Tinplate

31. **Wing pivot shaft (2)** ³⁄₃₂in brass rod

32. **Wing pivot shaft retainers (2)** ⅛in birch plywood

33. **Eggs (5)** 1in birch balls

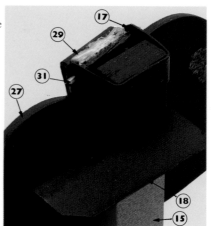

MAKING THE PARTS

1 Trace the templates and cut out the parts in the materials indicated using a fretsaw and tenon saw. Drill the marked holes in the bit size specified. When making two parts from the same template, tack or tape two sheets of plywood together and cut both pieces at the same time. Cut the head and beak pieces (8 and 10) as one piece and shape the front of the beak to a rounded point before separating them by cutting along the marked line.

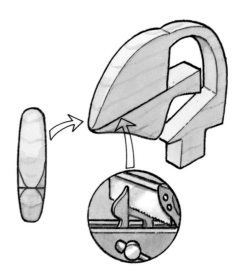

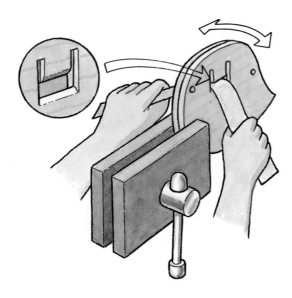

4 Cut the birch dowel to the lengths specified in the table. Sand, if necessary, so that the pieces fit snugly in the ¼-inch holes drilled in the body pieces.

Part (number)	Length
4. Spacers (× 3)	2¾in
5. Egg guides (× 2)	2in
20. Egg door push rod (× 1)	2½in
13. Beak push rod (× 1)	2⅜in

2 To ensure correct alignment of the holes in the inner (1) and outer (2) body pieces, tack these together in pairs with brads and drill through both pieces together. With the two outer body pieces tacked or taped together in a vise, shape the two outside edges of the wing pivot holes using a craft knife. Finish with sandpaper.

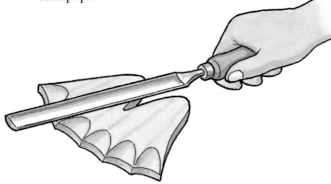

3 Shape the toes of the feet piece (19) with a rasp or coarse sandpaper wrapped around a 1-inch dowel.

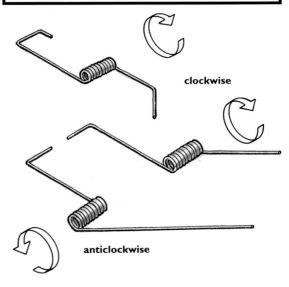

clockwise

anticlockwise

5 Hold a ³⁄₃₂-inch drill bit in a vise and make the beak pivot spring (12) and egg door springs (24 and 25) by winding piano wire around the bit shank in the directions shown for the spcified number of turns. When each spring is complete, remove from the bit and trim the ends to the required length and bend to the shape illustrated.

6 Use metal snips to cut out the brass sheet for two wing pivot shaft bearings (17). Then cut out the beak push rod plate (18), and drill the $\frac{3}{64}$-inch holes in all pieces, as indicated on the templates.

THE BODY CAVITY

The works and the chamber for the eggs are enclosed in a cavity between the inner and outer body side pairings and the surround.

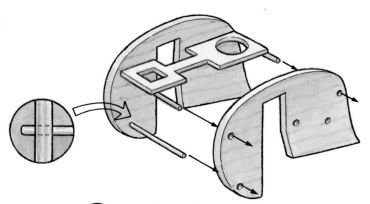

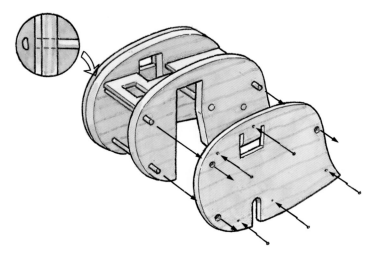

7 Chamfer both ends of the three spacers and insert them in the holes on the inner side of one inner body piece (1) so that the ends protrude by $\frac{3}{16}$ inch. Apply glue to the sides and underside of the egg tray (6), as shown, and position over the top spacers. Place the other inner body piece over the spacers so that the ends protrude as before. Make sure that the sides are parallel.

8 Chamfer one end of each egg guide. When the glue is dry, insert the egg guides in the remaining holes in the inner body pieces by pushing them, chamfered end first, from one side.

9 Apply glue to the outer surface of each inner body piece. Thread each outer body piece (2) over the protruding ends of the spacers of the corresponding inner body piece, making sure that the rounded side of the slot of each outer body piece is facing out. Attach with brads, supporting the assembly with scrap wood or over the corner of your workbench. Allow to dry, then cut off the protruding ends of the spacers on the outer sides of the body and sand smooth.

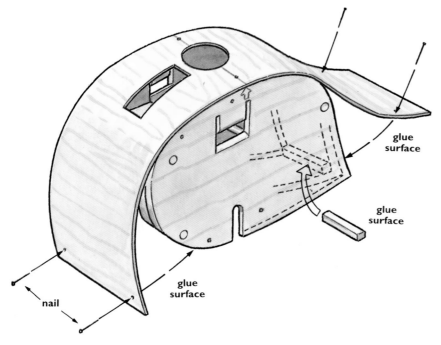

glue surface

glue surface

glue surface

nail

The head assembly is bold and bright and features a spring-loaded lower half to give the highly entertaining "squawking" effect.

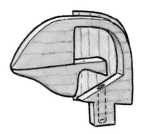

12 Drill a hole vertically through the center of the "neck" of the head (8), using a ¼in-inch bit. Glue one head side (9) to one side of the head, allowing the edges of the head side to protrude at the top and back of the head to allow for trimming later.

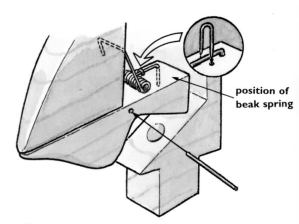

position of beak spring

10 Position the body surround (3) so that the center of the egg hole in the surround lines up with the point marked on the outer body pieces (2). When you are happy with the positioning, apply glue to the edges of the body pieces and attach the surround to the body with brads. Cut the tail brace (7) from scrap ⅜-inch birch plywood and glue between the body sides at the tail end.

11 When the whole assembly is dry, trim the surround flush with the body sides and tail with a craft knife and sand smooth.

13 Position the beak (10) inside the head. Using the existing hole in the beak as a guide, drill through the head side using a ¹⁄₁₆-inch bit. Press one end of the beak pivot spring (12) into the beak, as shown, and attach with a bent sewing pin. Insert the ¹⁄₁₆-inch rod for the beak pivot shaft (11) through the holes in the beak and head side.

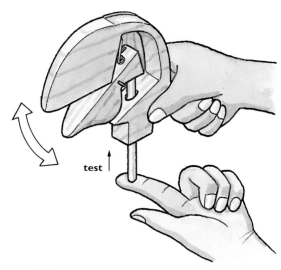

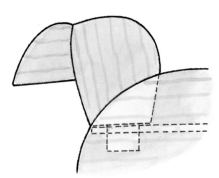

This assembly connects the wings with the legs and is also spring-loaded to make the wings flap when the bird is pressed down.

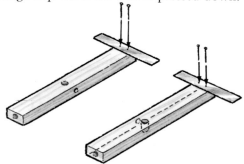

14 Insert the beak push rod (13) into the neck hole and check that it slides up and down freely, and that the beak opens and closes satisfactorily. Remove the beak and attach the other head side with glue. When dry, drill through the assembly with a $\frac{1}{16}$-inch bit to make the beak pivot hole. Trim the edges, sand, and then insert the beak mechanism and test the movement again.

15 Remove the beak and push rod. Slot the head assembly through the rectangular hole in the body to locate in the square hole in the egg tray and glue to secure. When dry, fill any gaps between head and body with auto-body filler.

16 Making sure that the screw holes in each leg are facing the right way, use brads to attach the two wing pivot shaft bearings (17) to the tops of the legs in the position indicated on the template. File off the points of the nails if they protrude.

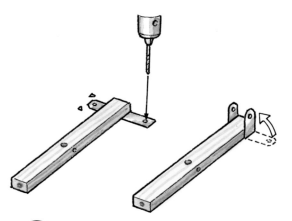

17 Drill holes in each end of the bearings with a $\frac{3}{32}$-inch bit, at a point $\frac{11}{16}$ inch from the edge of the wood. Snip off the corners of the bearings. Bend the sides of the bearings up, flush with the sides of the legs.

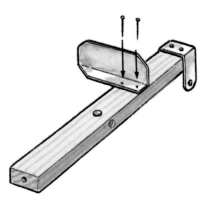

18 Bend the beak push rod plate (8) along the line marked on the template into a 90° angle. Attach with brads to the right leg (15) in the position shown on the template. Smooth all brass edges with a file.

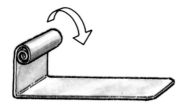

19 With a ³⁄₃₂-inch drill bit in a vise, coil one end of each wing bearing (29 and 30) around the shank three times with a pair of pliers. Bend each bearing to form a right angle at a point ¾ inch from the base of the coil.

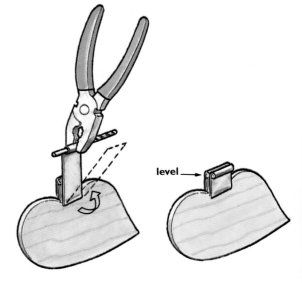

level →

20 Insert one of the bearings through the slot in one of the wings (27) and repeat this with the other wing from the opposite side. Working with each wing in turn in a vise, bend the bearings up and coil the free end around the drill bit as before, until it is even with the coil at the other end. Solder the coils together. File metal edges smooth.

21 Refit the beak parts and beak push rod. Insert the right leg (15) inside the body with the wing pivot shaft bearings protruding through the slot in the body and check that the beak push rod moves up and down when you push the leg. You may need to trim the push rod a little. Insert the left leg (16) and attach the feet with the 1½-inch screws.

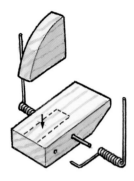

22 Glue the egg stop (22) to the egg door (21). Make the egg door pivot shaft (23) from a 2⅜-inch length of ³⁄₃₂-inch brass rod and thread this through the egg door. Place each egg door spring (24 and 25) over the ends of the shaft. Press the bent ends of each spring into the sides of the door.

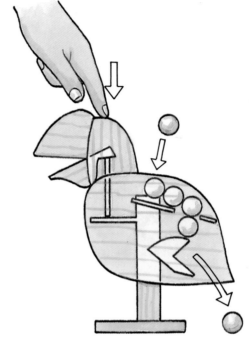

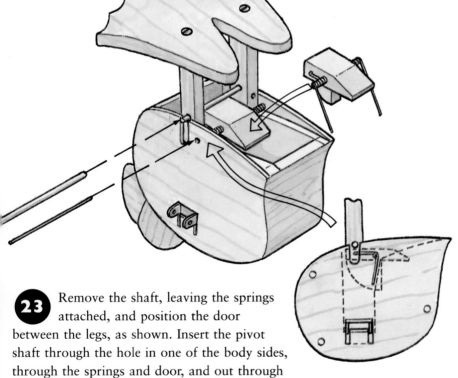

23 Remove the shaft, leaving the springs attached, and position the door between the legs, as shown. Insert the pivot shaft through the hole in one of the body sides, through the springs and door, and out through the other body side. Holding back the egg door, insert the egg door push rod (20) through the slot in the body sides and through the holes in both legs.

24 The egg door should now open when you push the legs. Put the five eggs (33) into the round hole in the top of the body, and press the bird down. An egg should come out of the egg door each time you do this. If you are happy with the way it works, attach the egg door push rod between the legs with the ½-inch screws inserted in the horizontal holes in the backs of the legs. Make sure that the sides of the legs do not rub against the body.

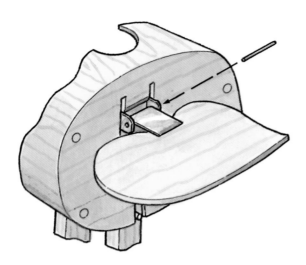

25 Cut two 1⅛-inch lengths of ³⁄₃₂-inch brass rod for the wing pivot shafts (31) and insert them through the wing pivot shaft bearings and the hole formed by the outer coil of the wing bearings. Check the troubleshooting box before painting.

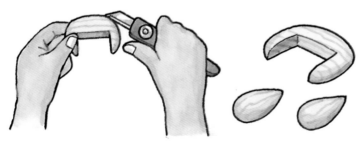

26 Remove the following parts: wing pivot shafts; egg door pivot shaft; leg and feet screws; legs; egg door; beak pivot shaft; beak and beak push rod. Shape the wing pivot shaft retainers (32) with a craft knife and coarse sandpaper as shown. Finish with fine sandpaper. Make two egg door pivot shaft retainers (26) from scrap softwood in the same way. Paint and varnish all parts to a hard-wearing finish (see Basic Techniques).

27 Reassemble when dry, adding the cheek pieces (14). After assembling the wings, glue the wing pivot shaft retainers and egg door pivot shaft retainers into position. Cover the screw holes with scrap dowel cut and sanded flush to the surface, and touch up the paintwork if necessary.

Troubleshooting

Fault	Cause	Remedy
Very stiff action	Legs rubbing against body	Reposition legs closer together
Eggs not coming down	Egg stop too big	Trim egg stop
Eggs jam inside	Egg stop too small	Remake larger
Puffin stops in "down position" (see fault 1)	Springs too weak; wings jamming	Increase strength of spring by bending; check wing bearings
Puffin hard to press down (see fault 1)	Springs too strong	Decrease strength of spring by bending
Beak opens too far or not enough	Beak push rod too short or too long	Trim or remake longer

· LION TAMER ·

This fascinating toy, based on a circus scene in which a lion tamer places his head inside a lion's mouth, is a simple automaton – a model with moving parts. In this case, the movement is produced by turning a handle which moves the interconnecting cog wheels and cams that turn the lion tamer and the lion. Toys of this kind need to be handled with care and are probably unsuitable for small children to play with unsupervised. The cog-wheel principle can be adapted for use in automation of your own design.

EQUIPMENT

Fretsaw

Tenon saw

Drill and bits
³⁄₆₄in, ¹⁄₁₆in, ³⁄₃₂in, ¼in

Mini drill chuck

Compass

Protractor

Wire cutters

Metal file

Small C-clamp

Needle- and round-nosed pliers

Screwdriver

Craft knife

MATERIALS

⅛in hardboard
8 × 6in

⅜in birch plywood
6 × 6in

⅛in birch plywood
6 × 6in

¹⁄₁₆in birch plywood
3 × 2in

⅞in softwood
6 × 6in

¼in birch dowel
12in

¹⁄₁₆in birch dowel
3in

¹⁄₁₆in copper-coated welding rod
6in

¹⁄₃₂in welding wire or brass rod
12in

Clear plastic sheet
1 × 1in

½in gimp tacks or brads
½oz

½in screws
(× 6)

¾in brass or mild steel brads
½oz

Sewing pins
(× 2)

Toy-safe paints

Varnish

Rapid-drying epoxy glue

Scrap plywood
3 × 3in

Scrap hardboard

The templates on this page are shown at 80 percent, or 4:5. The side elevation and templates on the following pages are full size.

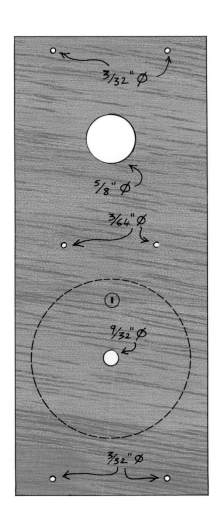

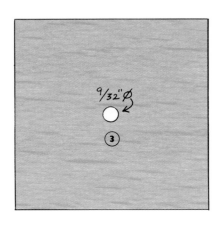

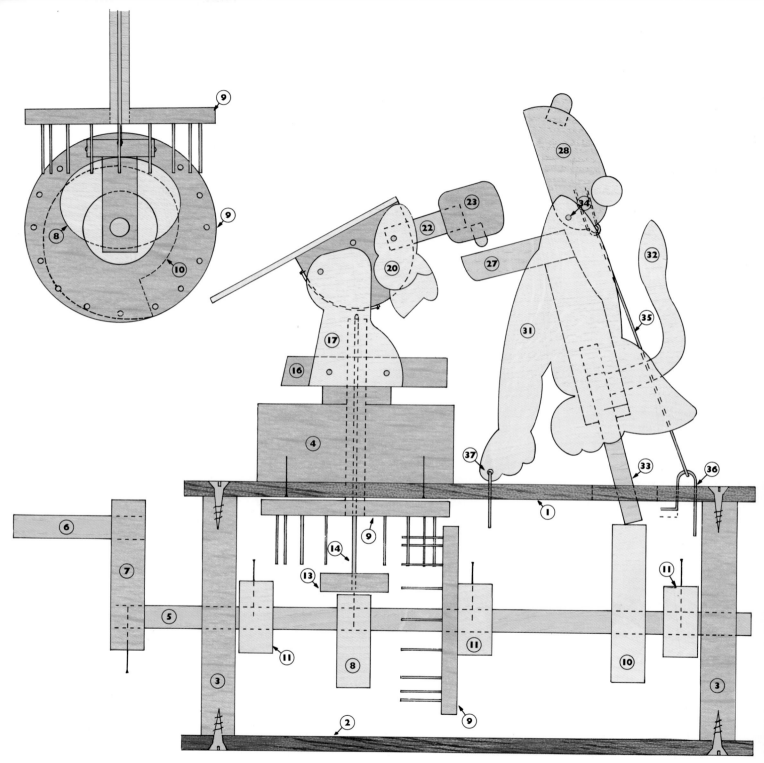

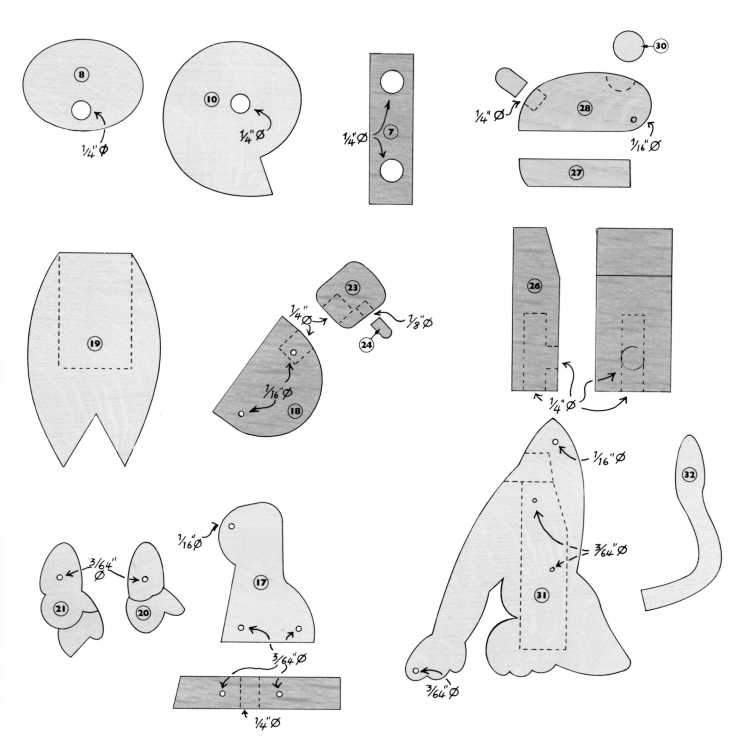

8

10

1/4"∅

1/4"∅

7

1/4"∅

30

28

1/4"∅

1/16"∅

27

19

23

1/4"∅

24

1/8"∅

18

1/16"∅

26

1/4"∅

1/16"∅

32

3/64"∅

31

21

3/64"∅

20

17

1/16"∅

3/64"∅

1/4"∅

3/64"∅

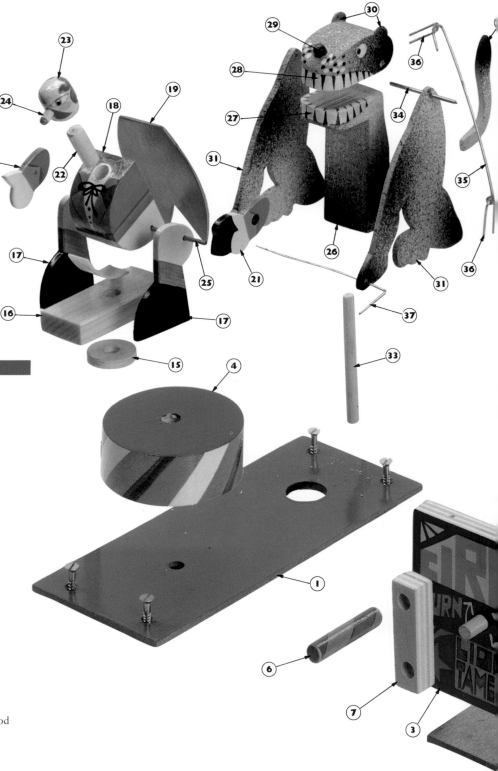

PARTS LIST

1. **Platform** Hardboard
2. **Base** Hardboard
3. **Side panels** (2) ⅜in birch plywood
4. **Tamer stand** Softwood
5. **Main shaft** ¼in birch dowel
6. **Handle** ⅜in birch plywood
7. **Handle shaft** ¼in birch dowel
8. **Tamer cam** ⅜in birch plywood
9. **Cog** (2) ⅛in birch plywood
10. **Lion cam** ⅜in birch plywood
11. **Collar** (3) ⅜in birch plywood
12. **Hollow shaft** ¼in birch dowel
13. **Cam follower** Scrap plywood
14. **Cam follower rod** ¹⁄₁₆in metal rod
15. **Spacer** ⅛in birch plywood
16. **Tamer base** Softwood
17. **Tamer leg** (2) ⅛in birch plywood
18. **Tamer body** Softwood
19. **Tamer coat-tails** ¹⁄₁₆in birch plywood

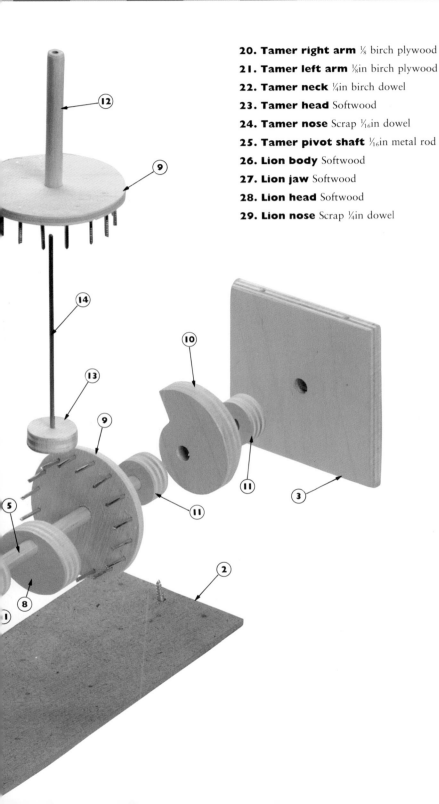

20. **Tamer right arm** ⅛ birch plywood

21. **Tamer left arm** ⅛in birch plywood

22. **Tamer neck** ¼in birch dowel

23. **Tamer head** Softwood

24. **Tamer nose** Scrap ¹⁄₁₆in dowel

25. **Tamer pivot shaft** ¹⁄₁₆in metal rod

26. **Lion body** Softwood

27. **Lion jaw** Softwood

28. **Lion head** Softwood

29. **Lion nose** Scrap ¼in dowel

30. **Lion ear** (2) ¹⁄₁₆in birch plywood

31. **Lion side** (2) ⅛in birch plywood

32. **Lion tail** ⅛in birch plywood

33. **Lion push rod** Scrap ¼in dowel

34. **Lion jaw pivot shaft** ¹⁄₁₆in metal rod

35. **Lion head stay** ³⁄₆₄in wire

36. **Lion head stay retainer** (2) ³⁄₆₄in wire

37. **Lion pivot shaft** ³⁄₆₄in wire

MAKING THE PARTS

Because of the complexity of the mechanism, take great care with the accuracy of the parts.

1 Trace the templates and mark each element, including the drill holes, on the type of wood indicated. Cut out all the pieces. Shape the softwood parts with a plane and sand all parts smooth. Drill the holes.

2 Cut the ¼-inch dowel into the following lengths: 7 inches; 2⅛ inches; 2 inches; 1⅜ inches; ⅞ inch; ⅜ inch. See the side elevation.

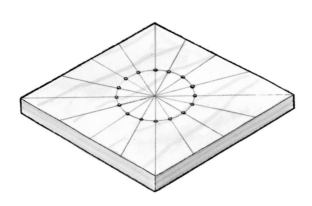

3 To make the cogs (9), first make a jig using a 4-inch square of scrap plywood. Find the center as shown and draw a circle with a diameter of $1^{11}/_{16}$ inches. Mark 16 radiating lines at 22.5° angles and drill holes in the positions indicated.

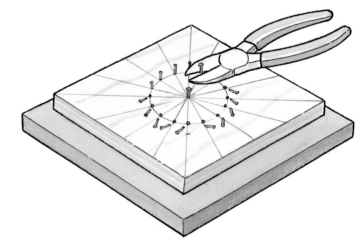

5 Hammer brads through the marked points on the jig and cog blank so that they protrude about $^1/_{16}$ inch into the hardboard. Snip off the heads of the pins close to the jig with wire cutters. Remove the center pin and gently separate the cog from the jig.

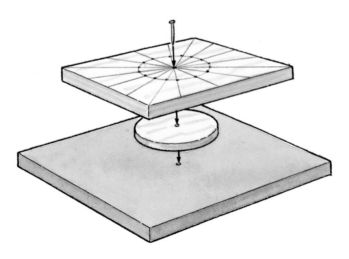

4 Attach a cog blank (9) underneath the jig, using a ¾-inch brass brad through the center of the jig and cog blank and onto a scrap of hardboard.

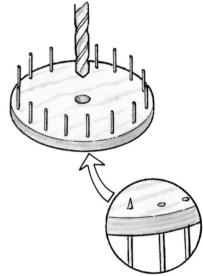

6 Drill the center hole of the cog with a ¼-inch bit and file the points of the cog pins smooth on the underside.

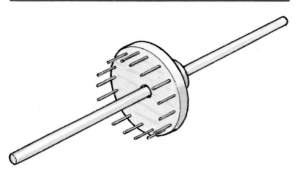

7 Push the main shaft (5) through the cog and glue the cog halfway along. Position a collar (11) behind the cog, and attach with a ¾-inch brad through the collar.

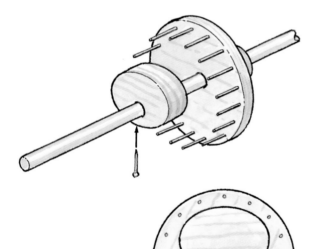

8 Place the tamer cam (8) on the shaft. Align the bottom of the cam with one of the cog teeth and mark the cog in pencil, as shown. Retain the cam with a gimp tack.

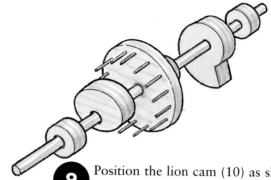

9 Position the lion cam (10) as shown and place the two end collars on the shaft. A tight but movable fit is important. Do not attach them, as they may need adjusting.

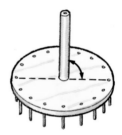

10 Make the second cog using the jig as before, and glue the hollow shaft (12) at right angles to the center of the cog, flush to the underside (see elevation).

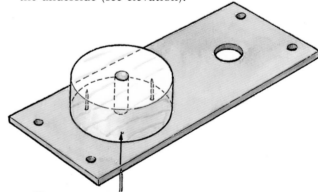

11 Nail the stand (4) to the top of the platform where shown, using three gimp tacks. Make sure the center hole of the stand aligns with the hole in the platform.

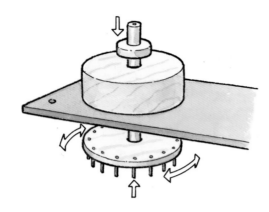

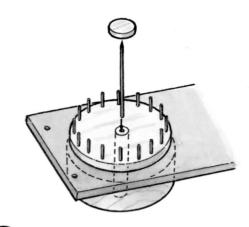

12 Insert the hollow shaft with cog attached through the hole in the platform and retain in position with the spacer (15), which should be a tight but movable fit. The cog and shaft should spin freely.

14 Insert the tamer cam follower rod (14) through the hole in the tamer cam follower (13) and glue. Place the rod through the hollow shaft (12).

15 Screw the platform to the side panels, making sure the rod does not fall out of the shaft, by holding it with fingers.

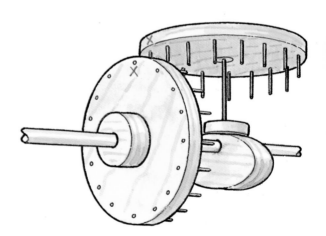

13 Place the side panels (3) of the stand on the main shaft and screw these to the base (2) as indicated. Make sure that the shaft spins freely. Slot pieces 6 and 7 together to make the handle and place on the end of the shaft, aligned to the tamer cam, as shown.

16 Mark on the tamer cog the point where it meets the pencil mark on the drive cog.

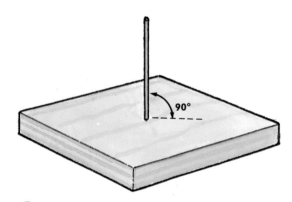

17 Make the jig for aligning the tamer's legs using a piece of $\frac{1}{16}$-inch dowel or wire rod fixed at right angles into a hole drilled in scrap $\frac{3}{8}$-inch plywood.

19 Glue the tamer's coattails (19) to the body (18), the neck (22) to the head (23), and the nose (24) to the head. Position the head on the body. Attach the piece of plastic to the body as shown with sewing pins trimmed to about $\frac{1}{4}$ inch.

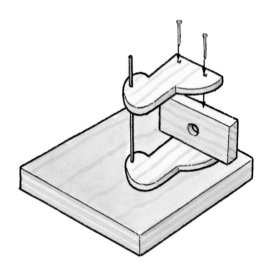

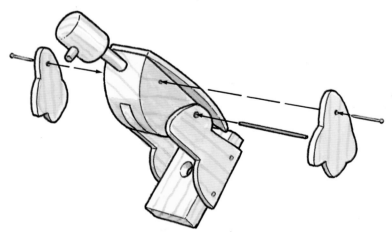

18 Nail the tamer's right leg (17) to the tamer base (16) using two gimp tacks. Place the assembly on the jig so that the rod passes through the hole in the leg. Position the left leg as shown and nail to the base. Remove the leg assembly from the jig.

20 Attach the arms (20 and 21) with gimp tacks, making sure (21) is on the left. Place the body between the leg assembly and thread the tamer pivot shaft (25) through the legs and body. Ensure that the parts swivel smoothly on the shaft.

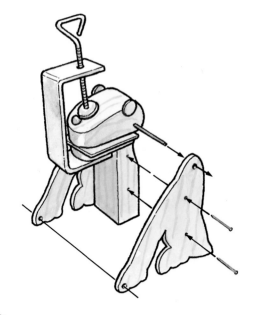

21 Glue the lion's lower jaw (27) to the lion's body (26). Drill two holes in the back of the lion's head, slightly to the left as shown, with a ³⁄₆₄-inch bit. Glue the ears (30) and the nose (29) to the head.

23 Thread the jaw pivot shaft (34) through the head pivot hole. Align the sides (31) on the shaft. Stand the assembly on a flat surface to ensure that the lower pivot holes also align. When positioned correctly, nail each side to the body with two gimp tacks.

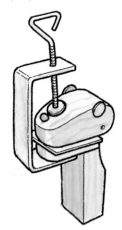

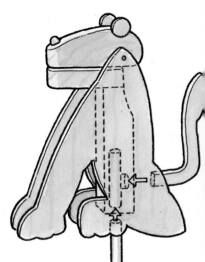

22 Clamp the head to the jaw, using a piece of thin posterboard as a spacer to ensure a good "snap" when the jaws open and close.

24 Glue the tail (32) in position, making sure it doesn't cover the push rod hole, and position the push rod (33).

25 Turn the handle of the main drive to the up position and then turn it so that the pencil marks are at opposite ends, as shown. Place the tamer assembly over the hollow shaft facing the handle end of the platform. Check that the tamer revolves properly and that he bends down as you turn the handle to the up position. You may need to unscrew the platform and shorten the cam follower rod to achieve this. When you are satisfied with the length, sand the top of the rod so that it is smooth and rounded.

26 Thread the lion pivot shaft (37) through the holes in its feet and bend the ends down as shown. Place the lion on the platform with the push rod passing through the hole in the platform so that it touches the lion cam. Pass the ends of the lion pivot shaft through the holes in the platform as shown and bend to secure.

27 Make the head stay (35) and the two head stay retainers (36) from the $\frac{1}{32}$-inch wire. Bend the ends of the head stay as shown so that its length is 2¾ inches. The head stay retainers are each approximately 1½ inches long. Bend one of the head stay retainers into a U-shape, insert the ends into the holes in the back of the lion's head, and push in firmly. Loop the squared end of the head stay through the retainer. Bend the second retainer into a U-shape. Attach it to the other end of the head stay and insert it through the holes in the platform, bending the ends underneath to secure.

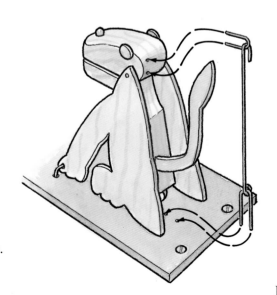

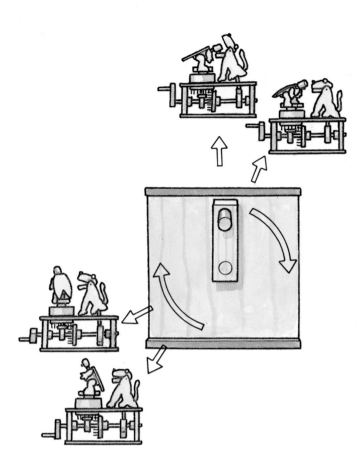

Fault	Cause	Remedy
Handle hard to turn	Main shaft bearing holes too small; not enough clearance between collars and sides	Enlarge with round file; reposition collars
Stiff cog action	Cogs not meshing properly; nails not straight	Try different mesh position; straighten nails
Tamer's head hits lion's head	Tamer bending down too far	Put pin stop in tamer body side to stop against leg
Tamer out of sync with lion	Tamer in wrong position on hollow shaft; lion cam in wrong position on main shaft	Readjust positions
Lion coming too far or not forward enough	Lion push rod too short or too long	Readjust length of push rod
Lion's mouth opens too little or too much	Head stay too long or too short	Adjust length of head stay

28 Check the timing of the mechanism. Adjust the tamer movement by rotating him on the hollow shaft. He should start to bend down when the handle reaches the 8 o'clock position and should be fully bent down and facing the lion at 12 o'clock. The lion should begin to open his mouth when the handle is at 7 o'clock; the mouth is fully open at 12 o'clock and snaps shut at 1 o'clock. Fine-tune the timing by adjusting the position of the lion cam on the main shaft. Check the troubleshooting box before painting.

PAINTING AND FINISHING

When you are satisfied with the assembly, mark the positions of all the adjustable parts and dismantle the assembly (apart from nailed and glued items). You will need to unscrew the platform.

29 Paint and varnish the parts individually as desired, except the works. Give all painted parts two coats of flat white, sanding between coats. The speckled appearance on the lion's head and body is achieved by flicking first brown and then cream paint with a toothbrush over a yellow ocher undercoat. When the head is dry, paint the eyes, nose, and teeth. The lion is not varnished. When all parts are dry, reassemble, attaching the adjustable parts with glue and brads.

· OFF-ROAD VEHICLE ·

Wheeled toys of all kinds are always popular, but the play value of this sturdy vehicle is enhanced by sophisticated features such as its independent suspension system, working winch, and flashing warning light.

The contrasting colors of the unpainted dark mahogany plywood and the pale birch plywood and dowel, together with the green painted bodywork, contribute to the rugged look of this versatile vehicle.

MATERIALS

½in Mahogany plywood
24 × 12in

½in birch plywood
12 × 6in

¼in birch dowel
24in

½in birch dowel
12in

Clear plexiglas or acrylic sheet
4 × 3in

6in nails
(× 4)

Galvanized roofing nut and bolt
¼ × 3½in

Nylon cord
7ft

⅜in flashing yellow LED (light-emitting diode)

Miniature push-button switch

9v battery (PP3) with connector and leads

High-pressure bicycle inner tube
6 × 1¼in

Rapid-drying epoxy glue

Toy-safe paints

1in brads
(× 20)

Sewing pins

Masking tape

Cardboard

EQUIPMENT

Fretsaw

Tenon saw

Hacksaw

2¼in hole saw

Drill and bits
¼in, ¹⁄₁₆in, ⁷⁄₃₂in, ⅛in, ³⁄₁₆in
Spade bits: ½in, ⅜in
Countersink bit

½in chisel

Craft knife

⁵⁄₁₆in round file

Soldering iron and solder

Wire cutters

Pliers

Compass

Hammer

Rasp

TEMPLATES AND PLANS

The parts on this and the following page are at 50 percent, or 1:2. Those on page 163 are full size.

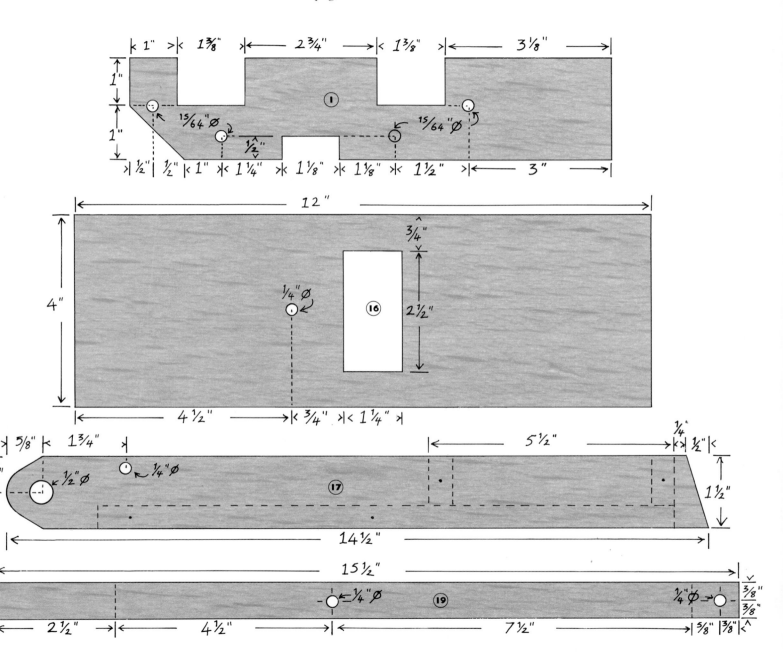

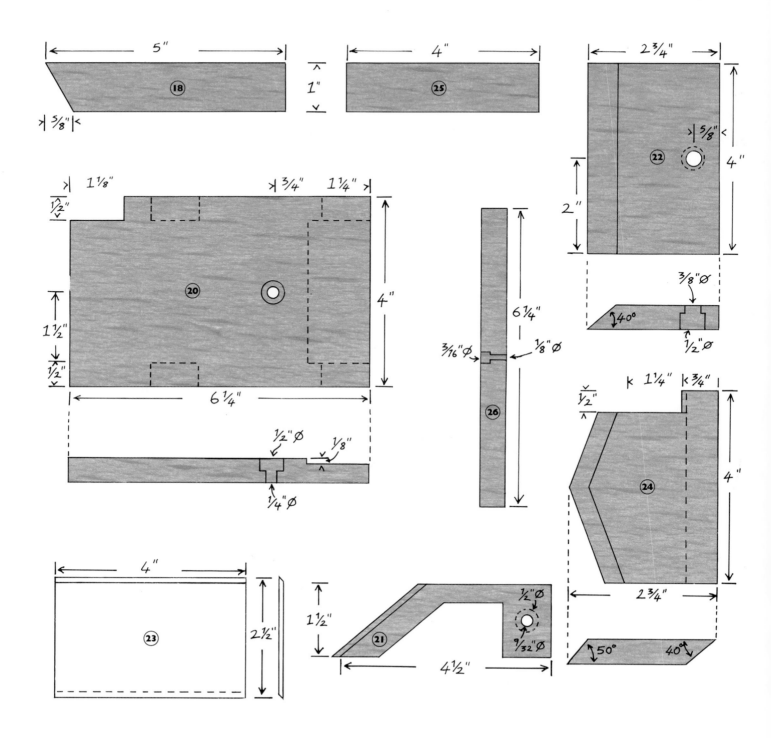

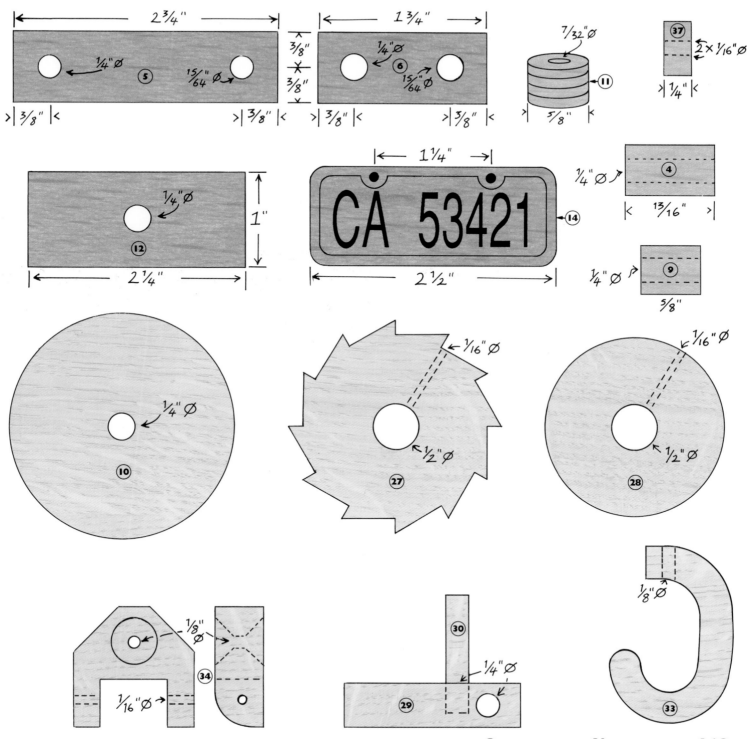

2¾"

1¾"

¼"∅
⑤
15/64"∅

3/8"
3/8"

3/8"
3/8"

3/8"
3/8"

¼"∅
⑥
15/64"∅

7/32"∅
⑪
5/8"

㊲
2 × 1/16"∅
¼"

¼"∅
⑫
1"
2¼"

1¼"
CA 53421
⑭
2½"

¼"∅
④
13/16"

¼"∅
⑨
5/8"

¼"∅
⑩

1/16"∅
½"∅
㉗

1/16"∅
½"∅
㉘

1/8"∅
㉞
1/16"∅

㉚
¼"∅
㉙

1/8"∅
㉝

PARTS LIST

1. **Chassis (2)** Mahogany plywood
2. **Suspension arm axle (2)** Nail
3. **Chassis band dowel (2)** ¼in birch dowel
4. **Chassis spacers (4)** ½in birch dowel

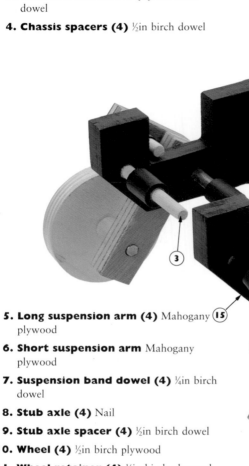

5. **Long suspension arm (4)** Mahogany plywood
6. **Short suspension arm** Mahogany plywood
7. **Suspension band dowel (4)** ¼in birch dowel
8. **Stub axle (4)** Nail
9. **Stub axle spacer (4)** ½in birch dowel
10. **Wheel (4)** ½in birch plywood
11. **Wheel retainer (4)** ½in birch plywood
12. **Clamp** Mahogany plywood
13. **Bolt** Galvanized roofing bolt
14. **Number plate** Mahogany plywood
15. **Bands (4)** Bicycle inner tube
16. **Floor** Mahogany plywood
17. **Sides (2)** Mahogany plywood
18. **Skirt (2)** Mahogany plywood
19. **Beam** Mahogany plywood

20. **Cab base** Mahogany plywood
21. **Cab window frame (2)** ½in birch plywood
22. **Cab roof** Mahogany plywood
23. **Windshield** Plexiglas/acrylic sheet
24. **Hood** Mahogany plywood
25. **Pick-up front and back (2)** Mahogany plywood
26. **Winch shaft** ½in birch dowel
27. **Winch ratchet** ½in birch plywood

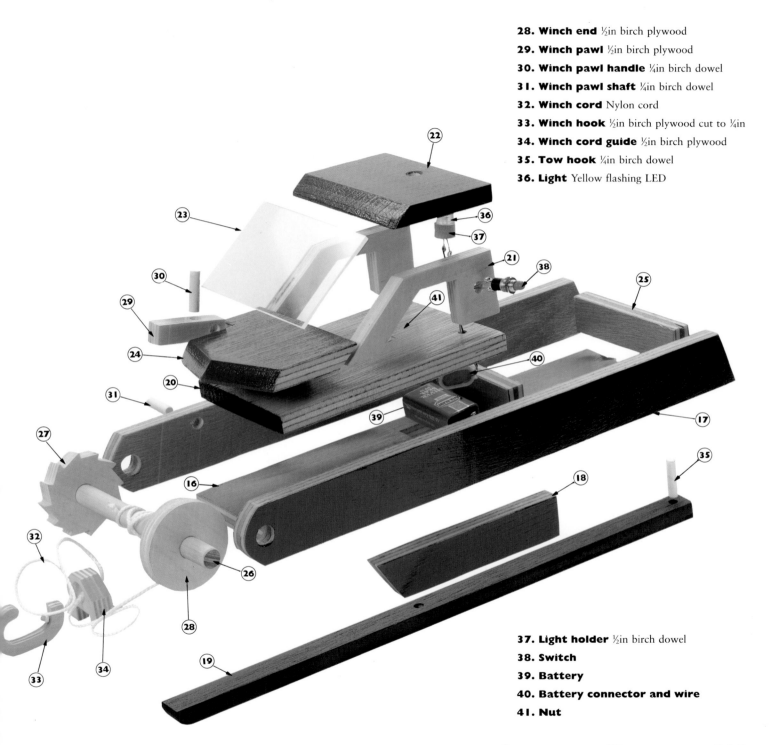

28. **Winch end** ½in birch plywood

29. **Winch pawl** ½in birch plywood

30. **Winch pawl handle** ¼in birch dowel

31. **Winch pawl shaft** ¼in birch dowel

32. **Winch cord** Nylon cord

33. **Winch hook** ½in birch plywood cut to ¼in

34. **Winch cord guide** ½in birch plywood

35. **Tow hook** ¼in birch dowel

36. **Light** Yellow flashing LED

37. **Light holder** ½in birch dowel

38. **Switch**

39. **Battery**

40. **Battery connector and wire**

41. **Nut**

OFF-ROAD VEHICLE • **165**

MAKING THE CHASSIS

1 Make templates for all parts indicated, and mark the positions of all the drill holes. Cut out all the parts in the type of wood indicated.

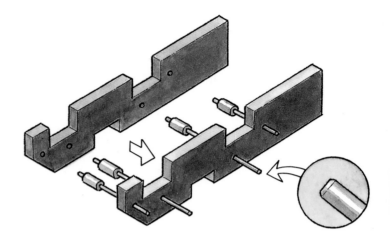

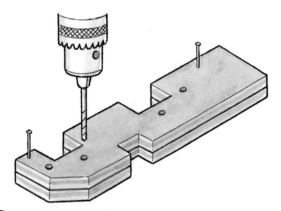

2 Nail the two chassis pieces (1) together with brads and drill the four holes indicated with a ¼-inch bit. Cut the two suspension arm axles (2) from two 6-inch nails to a length of 3¾ inches and two chassis band dowels (3) from ¼-inch birch dowel to a length of 3½ inches.

3 File the ends of the metal axles to remove any sharp edges. Paint the chassis sides black all over, and allow to dry.

4 Rest one of the chassis sides over a vise, as shown, using cardboard to protect the paintwork, and hammer the axles and dowels into the holes in one chassis side, as shown, so the axle ends protrude by 1 inch and the dowel ends by ¾ inch.

5 From the ½-inch birch dowel, cut four lengths of ¹³⁄₁₆ inch each for the chassis spacers (4). Drill a hole through the center of each with a ¼-inch bit. Paint black, and allow to dry. Put the spacers on the axles and dowels on the inside of the chassis. Hammer on the other chassis side so that the assembly is tight and the axle and dowel ends protrude by an equal amount on both sides.

MAKING THE SUSPENSION ARMS

6 Drill holes in the long and short elements of the suspension arms (5 and 6) as indicated on the template.

7 Make a jig by hammering part of a 6-inch nail through the center of a 3 × 3-inch piece of scrap plywood. Cut the head off the nail, which should protrude by 1½ inches.

8 Place one long suspension arm (5) on the jig with one of the holes over the nail. Then glue a short suspension arm (6) on top at 90° to the long arm. Drill two pilot holes through the short suspension arm with a ¹⁄₁₆-inch bit and hammer two brads through both pieces. Remove from jig and file off the points of the pins if they protrude.

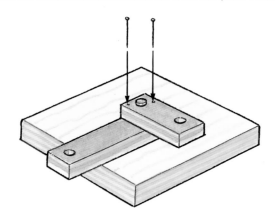

9 Assemble the remaining suspension arm pieces in the same way, ensuring that you make two assemblies with the short piece projecting to the right and two projecting to the left. Varnish and allow to dry.

10 Cut four 2-inch lengths from the nails and chamfer the ends to make the stub axles (8). Make the suspension band dowels (7) from 1¾-inch lengths of ¼-inch dowel. Hammer the axles and dowels into the suspension arms, as shown.

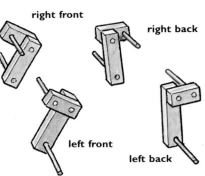

right front

right back

left front

left back

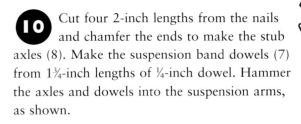

11 Draw four 2⅜-inch-diameter circles on the birch plywood, touching the edge, for the wheels (10). Drill a hole in the center of each wheel with a ¼-inch bit. Cut out wheels with the hole saw, sand, varnish, and allow to dry.

12 Make four stub axle spacers (9) from ⅝-inch lengths of ½-inch birch dowel. Drill a hole through the center of the axle spacers and wheel retainers (11) with a ¼-inch bit. Varnish the spacers and allow to dry. Paint the wheel retainers black.

13 Attach the wheels and spacers to the stub axles of the suspension arms, making sure that the wheels spin freely. Glue the retainers to the ends of the axles. Slot a scrap of thin cardboard between the retainer and the wheel to prevent the glue from coming into contact with the wheel. Lightly oil the axles.

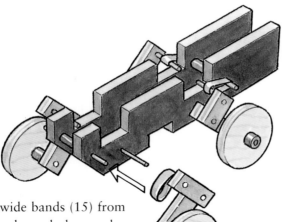

14 Cut four ½-inch-wide bands (15) from the bicycle inner tube and place each band over the suspension band dowels (7). Then insert the dowels through the holes in the chassis, as shown, looping the bands over the protruding ends of the chassis band dowels (2). Make sure that you place the suspension arms in the correct positions.

15 Paint the license plate, using red numbers on a white background, and varnish. When dry, nail it to the back of the chassis with two 1-inch brads. Drill the hole shown in the clamp (12), and varnish.

Making the Cab

16 Countersink a ⅛-inch hole on both sides of the winch cord guide (34). Shape one side as shown, to prevent the cord from rubbing. Drill the holes in the beam (19). Position the winch cord guide at the undrilled (front) end of the beam and use a rasp to round the beam flush with the cord guide. Separate the parts, paint the beam black, and varnish the cord guide. When dry, nail both pieces together with cut-down brads.

17 Cut a ⅞-inch length of ¼-inch birch dowel for the tow bar (35). Glue this into the hole in the end of the beam, pointing up and flush with the underside.

18 Cut the battery recess hole in the floor (16) with a fretsaw and drill the hole. Glue and nail the beam along the center of the floor, so that the measurement from the front of the winch cord guide to the front of the floor is 2½ inches.

19 Glue the skirts (18) to the underside of the side pieces (17) in the position indicated on the template guide.

20 Glue and nail the sides and skirts to the floor so that the distance from the curved front of the sides to the front of the floor is 1¾ inches. The undersides of the floor and sides should be flush. Make sure that the side with the extra hole (see template) is on the right. Glue the pick-up front and back (25) between the sides, resting on the floor. The distance between the pick-up front and the back of the floor should be 5½ inches.

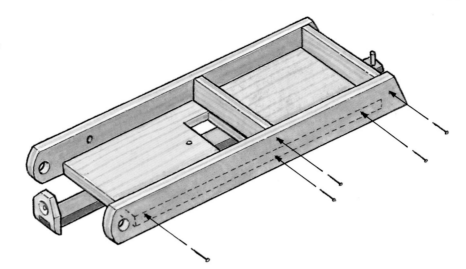

21 Paint the sides, skirts, and pick-up back green. Leave the edges unpainted. Varnish the whole assembly.

22 Make a recess in the underside of the cab base (20) in the position shown, by cutting through the first layer of plywood with a craft knife and chiseling away the excess. Place the nut from the roofing bolt in the recessed hole in the top of the cab base. This must be a tight fit; if it is loose, secure with rapid-drying epoxy glue.

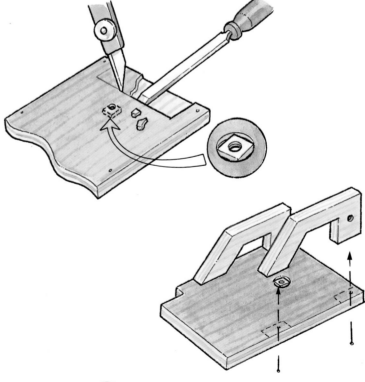

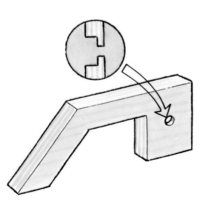

23 Drill a recessed hole for the light switch in one of the cab window frames (21) as shown. This piece becomes the left frame.

24 Glue the window frames to the cab base. Attach with cut-down brads hammered through the base into the frames, as shown. Varnish this assembly.

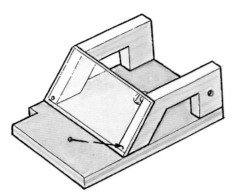

25 Cut a 2½ × 4-inch rectangle of plexiglas for the windshield (23) and use a metal file to chamfer the long sides to an angle of 40°. Drill two holes with a ¹⁄₁₆-inch bit on either side of the bottom edge, as shown, and nail it with brads to the window frames.

26 Chamfer the hood (24) and the front of the cab roof (22), as shown. Drill the recessed hole for the LED in the underside of the cab roof. Paint the hood (top and front) and roof (top, sides, front, and back) green, and then varnish and allow to dry.

27 Attach the assembly with brads. Working from underneath, nail the hood to the cab base, close to the windshield. Glue and nail the cab roof to the cab window frames.

MAKING THE WINCH

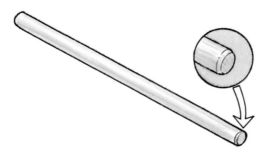

28 Cut a 6½-inch length of ½-inch birch dowel for the winch shaft (26) and round off the ends with sandpaper. Drill a recessed hole in its center as shown. Varnish and allow to dry.

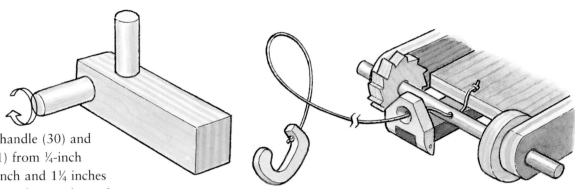

29 Cut the winch pawl handle (30) and winch pawl shaft (31) from ¼-inch birch dowel to lengths of 1 inch and 1¼ inches respectively. Enlarge the hole in the winch pawl (29) with a round file so that the shaft turns easily inside it. Drill a second hole in one side of the winch pawl with a ¼-inch bit to a depth of ¼ inch and glue the handle into this hole. Varnish this assembly and the following parts: winch ratchet (27), winch end (28), and winch hook (33). Allow to dry.

31 Thread the winch cord (32) through the winch cord guide and through the hole in the winch shaft. Knot at the shaft end and seal by melting the cord end with a lighted match. Thread the free end through the hole in the winch hook and tie a knot on both sides to secure. Seal the end as before.

32 Position the winch pawl assembly in the recess in the right side of the hood so that the hole for the shaft aligns with the hole in the right side piece. Hammer the winch pawl shaft through the hole, making sure that it is located in the hole in the winch pawl. Check that the winch works satisfactorily. Sand the exposed end of the shaft flush with the side; touch up the paint and varnish.

30 Put the winch shaft through the holes in the cab sides, making sure that it rotates freely. Thread the winch end and ratchet onto the shaft on each side of the central hole, as shown. These should be a tight but movable fit. Center the shaft between the sides and adjust the position of the winch end and rachet so that there is ¹⁄₁₆ inch of clearance between them and the sides. Attach with brads.

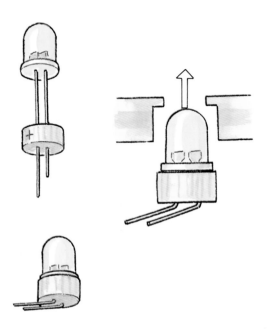

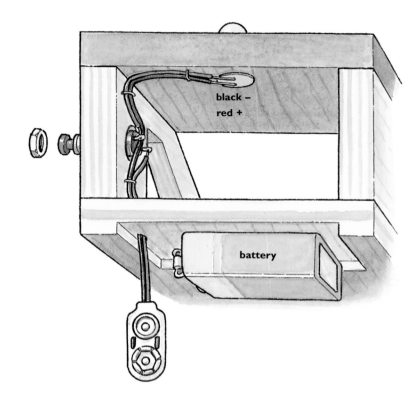

black –
red +

battery

33 For the light holder (37), cut a ¼-inch length of ½-inch birch dowel and drill two holes through the center with a ¹⁄₁₆-inch bit. Put the LED (36) in the holder, thread the two wires through the holes, and mark the hole through which the longer wire passes as positive (+). Trim both wires to ¼ inch and bend up flat. Mount the light and holder in the roof, with the positive (+) wire pointing toward the back of the cab.

34 Insert the switch (38) into the hole in the left window frame. Mark 1 inch along the wires from the battery connector. Thread the free ends of the wire through the hole in the cab base until the marked point is even with the switch tags and cut the red (+) wire only at this point. Solder the stripped ends of the red wire to each of the protruding switch tags. Feed the black wire between the tags. Take both wires up the side of the window frame and across the cab roof, and cut them where they meet the LED wires. Strip the ends and solder to the wires, taking care to attach the red wire to the wire marked +. Connect the battery and test. The light should flash when you press the switch.

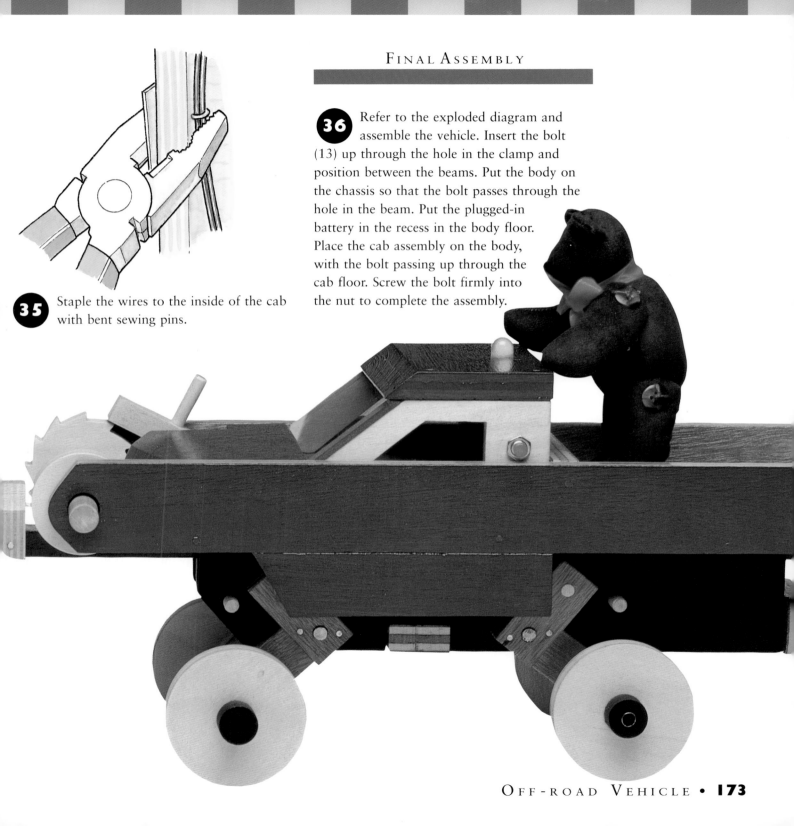

36 Refer to the exploded diagram and assemble the vehicle. Insert the bolt (13) up through the hole in the clamp and position between the beams. Put the body on the chassis so that the bolt passes through the hole in the beam. Put the plugged-in battery in the recess in the body floor. Place the cab assembly on the body, with the bolt passing up through the cab floor. Screw the bolt firmly into the nut to complete the assembly.

35 Staple the wires to the inside of the cab with bent sewing pins.

· INDEX ·